التوجيه الإلهي: فتح حكمة القرآن والحديث

Divine Guidance: Unlocking the Wisdom of Quran and Hadith

EBRAHIM ESSA

ابراهيم عيسى

بِسْمِ ٱللَّهِ ٱلرَّحْمَٰنِ ٱلرَّحِيمِ

In the name of Allah, the Most Merciful, the Most Compassionate.

لقد كتب هذا الكتاب خالصًا لمحبة الله ورحمته ورضوانه الذي أطلب منه بصدق أن يغفر ذنوب والدي وأختي وأهلي والمؤمنين الذين توفوا وأن يدخلهم جناته الأعلى.

This book was written purely for the love, mercy and pleasure of Allah who I sincerely ask to forgive the sins of my parents, sister, family and believers who have passed away and grant them entry to His highest eternal Garden of Paradise.

(سورة الإسراء 17:24)

وَقُل رَّبِّ ٱرْحَمْهُمَا كَمَا رَبَّيَانِى صَغِيرًا

"My Lord! Be merciful to them as they raised me when I was young."

(سورة الرعد 13: 24-23)

جَنَّـٰتُ عَدْنٍ يَدْخُلُونَهَا وَمَن صَلَحَ مِنْ ءَابَآئِهِمْ وَأَزْوَٰجِهِمْ وَذُرِّيَّـٰتِهِمْ ۖ وَٱلْمَلَـٰئِكَةُ يَدْخُلُونَ عَلَيْهِم مِّن كُلِّ بَابٍ سَلَـٰمٌ عَلَيْكُم بِمَا صَبَرْتُمْ ۚ فَنِعْمَ عُقْبَى ٱلدَّارِ

Gardens of Eternity, which they will enter along with the righteous among their parents, spouses, and descendants. And the angels will enter upon them from every gate, saying, "Peace be upon you for your perseverance. How excellent is the ultimate abode!

(سورة الفاتحة 1: 7-1)

بِسْمِ ٱللَّهِ ٱلرَّحْمَـٰنِ ٱلرَّحِيمِ

In the Name of Allah—the Most Compassionate, Most Merciful.

ٱلْحَمْدُ لِلَّهِ رَبِّ ٱلْعَـٰلَمِينَ

All praise is for Allah—Lord of all worlds.

ٱلرَّحْمَـٰنِ ٱلرَّحِيمِ

the Most Compassionate, Most Merciful,

مَـٰلِكِ يَوْمِ ٱلدِّينِ

Master of the Day of Judgment.

إِيَّاكَ نَعْبُدُ وَإِيَّاكَ نَسْتَعِينُ

You alone we worship and You alone we ask for help.

ٱهْدِنَا ٱلصِّرَٰطَ ٱلْمُسْتَقِيمَ

Guide us along the Straight Path.

أَنْعَمْتَ عَلَيْهِمْ غَيْرِ ٱلْمَغْضُوبِ عَلَيْهِمْ وَلَا ٱلضَّآلِّينَ

the Path of those You have blessed—not those You are displeased with, or those who are astray.

جدول المحتويات

مقدمة

Introduction

بِسْمِ ٱللَّهِ ٱلرَّحْمَـٰنِ ٱلرَّحِيمِ

In the name of Allah, the Most Merciful, the Most Compassionate

.والحمد لله رب العالمين. وأشهد أن لا إله إلا الله وأن محمداً عبده ورسوله

All praise and glory are due to Allah, the Lord of the Worlds. I bear witness there is no God but Allah and that Muhammad is his servant and Messenger.

(سورة الأنعام 6:153)

وَأَنَّ هَـٰذَا صِرَٰطِى مُسْتَقِيمًا فَٱتَّبِعُوهُ ۖ وَلَا تَتَّبِعُوا ٱلسُّبُلَ فَتَفَرَّقَ بِكُمْ عَن سَبِيلِهِ ۚ ذَٰلِكُمْ وَصَّىٰكُم بِهِ ۦ لَعَلَّكُمْ تَتَّقُونَ

Indeed, that is My Path—perfectly straight. *So, follow it and do not follow other ways, for they will lead you away from His Way. This is what He has commanded you, so perhaps you will be conscious of Allah."*

ن القرآن هو أعظم كتاب أدبي إسلامي في التاريخ، ولا يزال خاليًا من العيوب وسليمًا حتى اليوم تمامًا كما نزل منذ أكثر من ألف وأربعمائة عام.

The Quran is the greatest literary Muslim book in history and remains flawless and intact today exactly as it was revealed more than fourteen hundred years ago

(سورة الإسراء 17:88)

قُل لَّئِنِ ٱجْتَمَعَتِ ٱلْإِنسُ وَٱلْجِنُّ عَلَىٰٓ أَن يَأْتُوا بِمِثْلِ هَـٰذَا ٱلْقُرْءَانِ لَا يَأْتُونَ بِمِثْلِهِ ۦ وَلَوْ كَانَ بَعْضُهُمْ لِبَعْضٍ ظَهِيرًا

Say, O Prophet, "If all humans and jinn were to come together to produce the equivalent of this Quran, they could not produce its equal, no matter how they supported each other.

القرآن هو الأساس الأسمى للهداية الإلهية لكل مسلم. والحديث من جهة أخرى هو الحامل لسنة النبي صلى الله عليه وسلم. تعتبر قضية مثيرة للجدل بين العديد من المسلمين اليوم.

يعتقد المسلمون التقليديون أن الحديث مصدر تاريخي دقيق، يحافظ على أقوال النبي وأفعاله وموافقاته (عليه الصلاة والسلام). ومع ذلك، هناك بعض القرآنيين الذين يرفضون كل الحديث، ويدعون إلى اتباع نهج يتمحور حول القرآن.

Traditional Muslims believe that Hadith is an accurate historical source, preserving the words, actions and approvals of the Prophet (May the peace and blessings of Allah be upon him). There are however some Quranist that reject all Hadith, advocating for a Quran-centric approach.

The Quran is the supreme foundation of Divine guidance for every Muslim. Hadith on the other hand which is the carrier of the Sunnah of the Prophet (May the peace and blessings of Allah be upon him) is considered among many Muslims a controversial issue today.

يعتقد العلماء الغربيون، بما في ذلك المسلمون ذوو التفكير النقدي، أن نصوص الحديث لا يمكن إرجاعها بشكل موثوق إلى الكلمات الحرفية للنبي. (عليه الصلاة والسلام).

Western scholars including critical thinking Muslims believe that Hadith texts cannot be reliably traced back to the literal words of the Prophet (May the peace and blessings of Allah be upon him).

ويستند هذا الاعتقاد على المنهج النقدي التاريخي الذي يبحث في أصل النص الحديثي، وينظر إلى الأحداث التاريخية والثقافية في زمن كتابة الحديث.

لقد أحدثت الآراء المختلفة حول ضرورة وصحة الحديث في سياق القرآن ارتباكًا بين المسلمين مما أثار بعض الأسئلة المهمة

This belief is based on the historical critical method which investigates the origin of Hadith text, and looks at the historical and cultural events at the time Hadith was written.

The differing opinions on the necessity and reliability of Hadith in the context of the Quran have caused confusion among the Muslims which raised some important questions.

ماذا نحتاج الحديث عندما يكون لدينا القرآن؟ هل نتبع حديثاً يخالف آية من القرآن؟

هل النبي (عليه الصلاة والسلام) هل يتلقى الوحيغير القرآن؟

هل محمد هو آخر الأنبياء والرسل؟ لماذا ذكرت التوراة والإنجيل في القرآن؟

Why do we need Hadith when we have the Quran? Do we follow a Hadith that contradicts a verse of the Quran? Did the Prophet (May the peace and blessings of Allah be upon him) receive revelation other than the Quran?

Was Mohammad the last Prophet and Messenger? Why is the Torah and Gospel mentioned in the Quran?

جيب هذا الكتاب على بعض هذه الأسئلة وأكثر من خلال الاستشهاد بنصوص القرآن والحديث.

وأسأل الله العلي الرحيم أن يتقبل مني جهدي المتواضع، وأن يكون هذا الكتاب مصدر هداية ونفع للبشرية جمعاء.

والسلام عليكم ورحمة الله وبركاته محمد عبده ورسوله وأصحابه وسائر الأنبياء والمرسلين وأهليهم ومن تبعهم بإحسان

This book answers some of these questions and more through the citation of Quran and Hadith texts.

I ask Allah the Most High, the Most Merciful to accept my humble effort and that this book provides a source of guidance and benefit to all mankind.

May the peace and blessings of Allah be upon Muhammad his slave and Messenger, his companions, the other Prophets and Messengers, all their families and whosoever follows them in righteousness.

(سورة العنكبوت 29:69)

وَٱلَّذِينَ جَٰهَدُوا۟ فِينَا لَنَهْدِيَنَّهُمْ سُبُلَنَا ۚ وَإِنَّ ٱللَّهَ لَمَعَ ٱلْمُحْسِنِينَ

As for those who struggle in Our cause, We will surely guide them along Our Way. And Allah is certainly with the good-doers.

الفصل الأول
ضرورة الحديث

Chapter One
The Necessity of Hadith

(سورة النحل 16:44)

بِٱلْبَيِّنَـٰتِ وَٱلزُّبُرِ ۗ وَأَنزَلْنَآ إِلَيْكَ ٱلذِّكْرَ لِتُبَيِّنَ لِلنَّاسِ مَا نُزِّلَ إِلَيْهِمْ وَلَعَلَّهُمْ يَتَفَكَّرُونَ

We sent them with clear proofs and divine Books. And We have sent down to you O Prophet the Reminder, **so that you may explain to people what has been revealed for them, and perhaps they will reflect.**

(سورة آل عمران 3 :164)

لَقَدْ مَنَّ ٱللَّهُ عَلَى ٱلْمُؤْمِنِينَ إِذْ بَعَثَ فِيهِمْ رَسُولًا مِّنْ أَنفُسِهِمْ يَتْلُوا۟ عَلَيْهِمْ ءَايَـٰتِهِۦ وَيُزَكِّيهِمْ وَيُعَلِّمُهُمُ ٱلْكِتَـٰبَ وَٱلْحِكْمَةَ وَإِن كَانُوا۟ مِن قَبْلُ لَفِى ضَلَـٰلٍ مُّبِينٍ

Indeed, Allah has done the believers a great favor by raising a messenger from among them— **reciting to them His revelations, purifying them, and teaching them the Book** *and wisdom. For indeed they had previously been clearly astray.*

الحديث هو تقارير السنة النبوية عليه الصلاة والسلام و هذا يشمل أقوال وأفعال وتقاليد النبي محمد والتي تم استخدامها كمصدر رئيسي في الشريعة الإسلاميةاليوم.

Hadith is reports of the Sunnah of the Prophet (May the peace and blessings of Allah be upon him). This includes the sayings, actions and traditions of the Prophet Muhammad which have been used as a major source in Islamic law today.

سنة رسول الله صلى الله عليه وسلم هي مركبة الحديث. ولا يمكننا أن نفهم السنة إلا من خلال القرآن والحديث. أصل أي نص حديث يأتي من القرآن والسنة النبوية محمد.

The Sunnah of the Messenger of Allah (May the blessings and peace of Allah be upon him) is the vehicle of Hadith. We can only understand the Sunnah through the Quran and Hadith. The origin of any Hadith text comes from the Quran and the Sunnah of the Prophet Muhammad.

صلى الله عليه وسلم موعظة وجلت منها قلوبنا، وجلت منها أعيننا.قال أبو نجيح العرباض بن سارية رضي الله عنه : وعظنا رسول الله

قلنا: يا رسول الله! كأن هذه موعظة مودع فأوصنا». قال (صلى الله عليه وسلم): أوصيكم بتقوى الله، والسمع والطاعة لأميركم ولو أميركم عبد.

فإنه من يعش منكم فسوف يرى خلافا كثيرا كذلك فعليكم بسنتي وسنة الخلفاء الراشدين، الذين يرشدون إلى الطريق الصحيح.

التشبث به بعناد مع أسنانك المولية. "إياكم ومحدثات الأمور في الدين، فإن كل بدعة ضلالة"

رواه أبو داود والترمذي

Abu Najeeh al-Irbaad ibn Saariyah (May Allah be pleased with him) said: The Messenger of Allah (May the peace and blessings of Allah be upon him) gave us a sermon by which our hearts were filled with fear and tears came to our eyes.

So, we said, "O Messenger of Allah! It is as though this is a farewell sermon, so counsel us." He (May the peace and blessings of Allah be upon him) said, "I counsel you to have taqwa (fear) of Allah, and to listen and obey your leader even if a slave were to become your ameer.

Verily he among you who lives long will see great controversy, so *you must keep to my Sunnah and to the Sunnah of the Khulafa ar-Rashideen (the rightly guided caliphs),* those who guide to the right way.

Cling to it stubbornly with your molar teeth. Beware of newly invented matters in the religion, for verily every bidah (innovation) is misguidance."

Narrated by Abu Dawud as well at-Tirmidhi

أقسام الحديث حسب الرواة

Categories of Hadith based on Narrators

هناك ثلاث فئات من الحديث بناءً على الرواة المقبولين على نطاق واسع لدى المسلمين.

There are three categories of Hadith based on narrators which are widely accepted by Muslims.

الحديث القدسي

Hadith Qudsi (Sacred)

لحديث القدسي ينسب إلى الله مباشرة، حيث كان رسول الله صلى الله عليه وسلم يبلغ الرسائل من الله بالإلهام أو الحلم، ثم يبلغ المعنى للأمة بلسانه.

Hadith Qudsi is directly attributed to Allah where the Messenger of Allah (May the peace and blessings of Allah be upon him) would convey messages from Allah by way of inspiration or dream, and then communicate the meaning to the Ummah in his own words.

المتواتر

Mutawatir (Consecutive)

والحديث يعتبر صحيحا لأنه رواه جمع كثير من أصحاب النبي (عليه الصلاة والسلام). ومن الأمثلة العملية على الحديث المتواتر الحج والصيام والزكاة وتلاوة القرآن والصلوات الخمس.

Hadith is regarded as authentic because it was reported by a large number of companions of the Prophet (May the peace and blessings of Allah be upon him). A practical example of the Mutawatir Hadith is Hajj, fasting, Zakat, recitation of the Quran and practices of the five daily prayers.

إن عدد الأحاديث الشفوية المتواترة المنسوبة إلى النبي قليل ومشكوك فيه، حيث لا يوجد إجماع بين العلماء على عدد محدد.

The number of verbal Mutawatir Hadith attributed to the Prophet is few and questionable as there is no consensus amongst scholars as to an exact number.

معزول

Ahad (Isolated)
أحاديث لا يصل عددها إلى النقل الجماعي للأحاديث المتواترة. ويصنف الحديث كذلك إلى غريب ونادر ومشهور.

Hadith whose numbers do not reach the mass transmissions of that of Mutawatir Hadith. Hadith is further classified into strange, rare and famous.

غريب

Gharib (Strange, scare)
يرويه راوٍ واحد في أي مرحلة من مراحل الإسناد. سلسلة السلطة

A single transmitter of Hadith narrates it at any stage of the isnad. (chain of authority)

عزيز

Aziz (Strong, rare)
ورواه اثنان من الرواة في أي مرحلة من الإسناد. سلسلة السلطة

Two transmitters of Hadith narrate it at any stage of the isnad. (chain of authority)

مشهور

Mashhur (Famous)
ويوجد للحديث أكثر من اثنين يرويانه في أي مرحلة من مراحل الإسناد. سلسلة السلطة

There are more than two transmitters of Hadith who narrate it at any stage of the isnad. (chain of authority)

تصنيفات الحديث

Classifications of Hadith

تصنيف الأحاديث سواء كانت صحيحة أو جيدة أو ضعيفة أو موضوعة يعتمد على صدق الرواة وورعهم وعلمهم واستقامتهم وحسن حفظهم. ويجب أن تكون سلسلة الروايات والنصوص كاملة وغير منقطعة وموثوقة ومثبتة مع الرواة الآخرين.

The classification of Hadith whether they are Sahih, Hasan, Da'if or Mauda depended on the trustworthiness, piety, knowledge, integrity and good memory of the transmitters. The chain of narrations and text must also be complete, uninterrupted, reliable and must be corroborated with other transmitters.

صحيح

الحديث مع سلسلة كاملة وموثوقة وغير منقطعة من النقل والنص. ويجب أن يكون المرسلون معروفين بالصدق والعلم والتقوى والنزاهة وحسن الحفظ.

Sahih (Sound)

Hadith with a complete, reliable and uninterrupted chain of transmission and text. The transmitters must also be known for their honesty, knowledge, piety, integrity and good memory.

حسن

حديث بسند ناقص، أو برواية مشكوك في صحتها أو حفظها. والحديث كافٍ ليكون دليلاً.

(Hasan (Good

Hadith with an incomplete chain of transmission or with transmitters whose authority or memory is questionable. The Hadith is sufficient to be used as supporting evidence.

ضعيف

لحديث حيث يتعرض المرسلون أو المتن لانتقادات خطيرة. ومثال ذلك ما كان معروفا عن الرواة أنهم يكذبون أو يخطئون كثيرا أو يخالفون روايات الثقات

Da'if (Weak)

Hadith where the transmitters or matn (text) are subject to serious criticism. An example is where the transmitters are known to tell lies, make excessive mistakes or oppose the narrations of more reliable trustworthy transmitters.

مودو (ملفقة، مزورة)

نص الحديث يتعارض مع تواريخ وأوقات تقرير حديث معين. ولفظه أيضاً مخالف للحديث الصحيح.

Maudu (Fabricated, forged)

The text of the Hadith goes against the dates and times of a particular Hadith reporting. The wording is also opposite to that of an authentic Hadith.

التركيز الرئيسي للمسلمين بعد وفاة النبي (صلى الله عليه وآله وسلم) كان القرآن. ويرجع ذلك إلى حد كبير إلى جهود أصحاب النبي وهم أبو بكر وعمر وعثمان وعلي (رضي الله عنهم) الذين أجبروا الناس على اتباع القرآن مع الحد من انتشار الحديث.

The main focus for Muslims after the death of the Prophet (ﷺ) was the Quran. This was largely due to the efforts of the companions of the Prophet namely Abu Bakr, Umar, Uthman and Ali (May Allah be pleased with them) who compelled people to follow the Quran while reducing the spread of Hadith.

ولم يرد أصحاب النبي أن يخلط المؤمنون بين آيات القرآن وآيات الحديث.

The companions of the Prophet did not want the believers to confuse the verses of the Quran with that of Hadith.

وبعد وفاة النبي صلى الله عليه وسلم جمع أبو بكر الناس فقال: إنكم تحدثون عن رسول الله صلى الله عليه وسلم أحاديث متناقضة. الأشخاص الذين يأتون بعدك سوف ينخرطون في تناقض أكثر حدة.

فلا تحدثوا عن رسول الله شيئا، وإذا سألك أحد فارجع إلى كتاب الله حكما. ولذلك يجب عليك أن تعتبر كل ما هو قانوني حلالاً فيها ويحرم ما هو محرم فيها

Al-Dhahbiy رواه

After the demise of the Holy Prophet, Abu-Bakr gathered people and said, 'You are reporting about the Messenger of Allah inconsistent narrations. People coming after you will be engaged in more intense discrepancy.

Therefore, do not report anything about the Messenger of Allah, and if anyone asks you, you should refer to the Book of Allah as the arbitrator.

You should thus deem lawful whatever is lawful therein and deem unlawful whatever is unlawful therein.

Narratted by Al-Dhahbiy

عمر في عهده كخليفة لم يسمح لأصحاب النبي (عليه الصلاة والسلام) أن يسافروا بحرية دون إذنه لأنه لا يريدهم أن ينشروا الحديث. رفع عثمان قيود السفر عندما أصبح الخليفة التالي.

أصحاب النبي (عليه الصلاة والسلام) يحب عبد الله بن عباس، وأنس بن مالك، وأبو هريرة، وعبد الله بن مسعود، وغيرهم توثيق الأحاديث.

Umar during his reign as Caliph did not allow the companions of the Prophet (May the peace and blessings of Allah be upon him) to travel freely without his permission because he did not want them to spread Hadith. Uthman lifted the travel restrictions when he became the next Caliph.

The companions of the Prophet (May the peace and blessings of Allah be upon him) like Abdullah ibn Abbas, Anas ibn Malik, Abu Hurayrah, Abdullah ibn Masud and others documented Hadiths.

قال أبو جحيفة رضي الله عنه:

فقلت لعلي (رضي الله عنه): هل عندك علم الوحي الإلهي غير ما في كتاب الله؟ فأجاب علي: لا, والذي فلق الحبة وخلق الروح. لا أعتقد أن لدينا مثل هذه المعرفة، ولكن لدينا القدرة على الفهم التي قد يمنحها الله للإنسان حتى يفهم القرآن، ولدينا ما هو مكتوب في هذه الورقة أيضًا.

انا سألت، "ما هو مكتوب في هذه الورقة؟" قال: الفهم، وإطلاق الأسير، وعدم قتل مسلم بكافر.

رواه البخاري

Abu Juhaifa (May Allah be pleased with him) said:

I asked Ali (May Allah be pleased with him) "Do you have the knowledge of any Divine Inspiration besides what is in Allah's Book?"

Ali replied, "No, by Him Who splits the grain of corn and creates the soul. I don't think we have such knowledge, but we have the ability of understanding which Allah may endow a person with, so that he may understand the Quran, and we have what is written in this paper as well."

I asked, *"What is written in this paper?"* He replied, "The understanding, releasing of the captive, and that a Muslim should not be killed by a disbeliever.

Narrated by Al-Bukhari

الإجماع بين أصحاب النبي (عليه الصلاة و السلام) وكان المسلمون يعتقدون أن الحديث يجب أن يتم تعلمه عن طريق الحفظ والكلام الشفهي. وتحول هذا إلى نص مكتوب عندما كان يخشى أن ينسى من ليس لديه ذاكرة جيدة روايات الحديث.

The consensus among the companions of the Prophet (May the peace and blessings of Allah be upon him) and Muslims was that Hadith should be learned through memorization and word of mouth. This changed to written text when it was feared that those who did not have a good memory would forget the Hadith narrations.

وعن الفضيل بن الحسن بن عمرو بن أمية عن أبيه قال:
حدثت أبا هريرة بحديث فنكره. فقلت: سمعته منك. وقال أبو هريرة :"إذا سمعت ذلك مني فيجب أن أكتبه". ثم أخذني إلى منزله، فأظهر لي كتباً فيها أحاديث كثيرة عن النبي صلى الله عليه وسلم، فوجد ذلك الحديث.
فقال أبو هريرة: كما قلت، إن كنت قد حدثتك فقد كتب هذا الحديث عندي.
رواه ابن عبد البر

Fudhayl ibn Ḥasan ibn ʿAmr ibn Umayyah narrated from his father who said

I told Abu Hurayrah about a hadith and he denied it. I said, "I heard it from you." Abu Hurayrah said, *"If you heard it from me I must have it written."* He then took me to his house, he showed me books containing many Hadith of the Prophet and he found that Hadith.

ABU HURAYRAH THEN SAID, "As I said, if I have ever told you, that hadith is recorded in mine.

Narrated by Ibn Abd al-Barr

أقدم مخطوطة للحديث هي صفحة واحدة من الموطأ للإمام مالك يرجع تاريخها إلى 179. هجرية

أدى التنافس بين الأمويين والعباسيين إلى إنشاء جمع الحديث.

استخدمت الأسرة الأموية الحديث كسلاح سياسي أقوى لفرض وتوسيع حكمها على قارات أوروبا وآسيا وأفريقيا. ضمت هذه القارات أعدادًا كبيرة من الأشخاص ذوي الخلفيات الثقافية والعرقية والدينية المتعددة.

The earliest manuscript for Hadith is a single page of the Muwatta by Imam Malik dating to 179AH.

The rivalry between the Umayyad and Abbasids led to the creation of the compilation of Hadith.

The Umayyad dynasty used Hadith as their most powerful political weapon to enforce and expand their rule over the continents of Europe, Asia and Africa. These continents included vast populations of people with multi-cultural, ethnic and religious backgrounds.

وأدى ذلك إلى تجميع العديد من الأحاديث التي أصبحت مزورة في المناقشات الفقهية والمذهبية والعقائدية. كما أنها خلقت فرصة ودافعًا لإنشاء مادة حديثية جديدة بسبب الأيديولوجيات الطائفية والقبلية والعقائدية المتضاربة والمتنافسة في ذلك الوقت.

وقد فتح هذا الباب أمام تلفيق الأحاديث على نطاق واسع حيث لم تكن هناك تدابير رقابية مثل تاريخ التقاليد العلمية الراسخة للتحقق من نقل الحديث والتحقق منه والتصديق عليه

This led to the compilation of many Hadiths which became forged in legal, sectarian and theological debates. It also created an opportunity and motivation for the creation of new Hadith material due to the conflicting and competing sectarian, tribal and theological ideologies at the time.

This opened the door for the mass fabrication of Hadiths as there were no control measures like a history of established scholar traditions in place to check, verify and authenticate the transmission of Hadith.

لقد تزايدت مع مرور الوقت تلفيق الأحاديث المنسوبة إلى ابن عباس (رضي الله عنه). عدد الأحاديث التي وردت عن ابن عباس ألف وستمائة وستين حديثا. وذلك مع مراعاة ما ورد من تسعة أو عشرة أحاديث سمعها ابن عباس من النبي صلى الله عليه وسلم (عليه الصلاة والسلام) وروايته لما قاله النبي مقابل الحديث الذي سمعه من سائر الصحابة.

The fabrication of Hadiths attributed to Ibn Abbas (May Allah be pleased with him) have significantly increased over time. The number of Hadiths reportedly attributed to Ibn Abbas is one thousand six hundred and sixty Hadiths.

This is taking in account the report of nine or ten Hadiths ibn Abbas actually heard from the Prophet (May the peace and blessings of Allah be upon him) and his report on what the Prophet said versus the Hadith narration he heard from the other companions.

ابن عمر (رضي الله عنه) له ألفان وستمائة وثلاثون حديثا، ويعتبر ثاني أكثر الرواة حديثا بعد أبي هريرة (رضي الله عنه).

الحديث التالي يخالف رواية ابن عمر روى أحاديث كثيرة.

وعن عبد الله بن أبي صفر قال: سمعت الشعبي يقول: "جلست مع ابن عمر سنة فلم أسمعه يحدث عن رسول الله صلى الله عليه وسلم شيئا الله (عليه الصلاة والسلام)"

رواه ابن ماجه

Ibn Umar (May Allah be pleased with him) had two thousand six hundred and thirty Hadiths attributed to him and are considered the second most prolific Hadith narrator after Abu Hurayah (May Allah be pleased with him)

The following Hadith contradicts the narrative that Ibn Umar narrated many Hadiths.

It was narrated that Abdullah bin Abu Safar said: "I heard Ash-Sha'bi saying: *I sat with Ibn Umar for a year and I did not hear him narrate anything from the Messenger of Allah (ﷺ)*"

Narrated by Ibn Majah

الحاجة إلى سلسلة الرواة

The need for Isnads

الحاجة إلى الإسناد (سلسلة الرواة) كعامل محدد لموثوقية ومصداقية الحديث نشأت فقط خلال الفتنة الثانية.

وكانت هذه فترة الاضطرابات والاضطرابات المدنية والسياسية والعسكرية خلال الخلافة الأموية المبكرة.

The need for Isnads (chain of narrators) as a determining factor for the reliability and credibility of Hadith only arose during the Second Fitna.

This was the period of civil, political and military unrest and turmoil during the early Umayyad Caliphate.

حدثنا أبو جعفر محمد بن الصباح، حدثنا إسماعيل بن زكريا، عن عاصم الأحول، عن النبي صلى الله عليه وسلم. قاله ابن سيرين: ولا يسألون عن الأسانيد, ولما وقعت الفتنة قالوا: سموا لنا رجالكم. فينظر إلى أهل السنة فيؤخذ حديثهم، ويعتبر أهل البدع ولا يؤخذ حديثهم».

رواه مسلم

Abu Ja'far Muhammad bin us-Sabbah narrated to us, Ismail bin Zakariyya narrated to us, on the authority of Asim il-Ahwal, on the authority of *Ibn Sirin that he said:*

"They would not ask about the chains of narration, and when the Fitnah occurred, they said: "Name for us your men". So Ahl us-Sunnah would be regarded, and their Ḥadith were then taken, and Ahl ul-Bi'dah (Innovators) would be regarded, and their Ḥadith were not taken".

Narrated by Muslim

بدأ تدوين الحديث في القرن الثامن في عهد عمر بن عبد العزيز الذي كان له تأثير إيجابي هائل على الإمبراطورية الإسلامية خلال العصر الأموي.

يعتبر عمر بن عبد العزيز نتيجة لتغيراته التحولية الرؤيوية في التاريخ الإسلامي أحد أنبل الحكام، حيث جاء في المرتبة الثانية بعد الخلفاء الراشدين الأربعة أبي بكر (وعمر وعثمان وعلي (رضي الله عنهم وكانت القاعدة في ذلك الوقت أن الإسناد يجب أن يكون موثقا كاملا، وأن يكون .الرواة معروفين بالعلم والتقوى والنزاهة وحسن الحفظ

The codification of Hadith started in the eighth century during the reign of Umar bin Abdul Aziz who made a monumental positive impact on the Muslim empire during the Umayyad period.

Umar bin Abdul Aziz as a result of his visionary transformative changes are considered in Muslim history as one of the most noble rulers, second only to the four rightly guided caliphs Abu Bakr, Umar, Uthman and Ali (May Allah be pleased with them)

The rule at the time was that the Isnad (chain of narrations) must be corroborated, complete and that the narrators were known for their knowledge, piety, integrity and good memory.

كما يجب ألا يتعارض الحديث مع القرآن وغيره من الأحاديث الصحيحة.لكن .القاعدة كانت ضعيفة لعدم وجود نقد لمضمون الحديث نفسه كانت نزاهة الرواة وتقواهم ومعرفتهم موضع تقدير كبير وبالتالي لم يتم التشكيك .فيها. وهذا أدى إلى عدم قيام أحد بالفحص والتشكيك في مضمون الحديث نفسه ونظراً لجهود علماء المسلمين الأوائل في توثيق الحديث، ومن نقل الحديث (اليوم فلا يفعله إلا وذكر إسناده. (سلسلة الروايات

The Hadith should also not contradict the Quran and other authentic Hadiths.*The rule however was weak because there was no criticism of the contents of the Hadith itself.*

The integrity, piety and knowledge of the narrators was held in high esteem and therefore not questioned. This led to no one examining and questioning the contents of the Hadith itself.

Due to the efforts of the early Muslim scholar's corroboration attempts to authenticate Hadith, *anyone citing Hadith today will not do so without mentioning its Isnad.* (chain of narrations)

أدى هذا التأييد إلى أصل ستة كتب حديثية قبلها المسلمون اليوم كمصدر أساسي (.منسوب للسنة النبوية (عليه الصلاة والسلام

أبرز علماء الحديث هما البخاري ومسلم الذين يمكن اعتبارهم نقاد الحديث بسبب
معاييرهم الصارمة في سلسلة الرواة

يعتبر صحيح البخاري وصحيح مسلم اليوم من أصح الأدب الإسلامي بعد القرآن
الكريم. أما الكتب الأربعة الأخرى فهي من سنن أبي داود، سنن النسائي، سنن ابن
ماجه وجامع الترمذي.

وتختلف أدبيات كتب الأحاديث الستة في درجة صحتها، فبعضها صحيح، وبعضها
الآخر له روايات متضاربة، وهي عموما مليئة بالتناقضات.

This corroboration led to the origin of six Hadith books which Muslims today have accepted as the primary source attributed to the Sunnah of the Prophet (May the peace and blessings of Allah be upon him).

The two most prominent scholars of Hadith are Al-Bukhari and Muslim who can be considered Hadith critics due to their strict criteria of chain of narrators.

Sahih Al-Bukhari and Sahih Muslim are today considered the most authentic Islamic literature after the Quran. The other four books are from Sunan Abi Dawud, Sunan al-Nasa`i, Sunan Ibn Majah and Jami al-Tirmidhi.

The literature from the six Hadith books differ in their degree of authenticity as some are authentic, others have conflicting narrations and are generally full of contradictions

يعتقد المسلمون التقليديون أن الحديث مصدر تاريخي موثوق للغاية. يعارض
علماء التاريخ النقدي العلماني هذا بشدة لدرجة أن الكثيرين يرفضون روايات
الحديث لأنه لا يمكن إرجاعها بشكل موثوق إلى الكلمات الفعلية للحديث. نبي (عليه
الصلاة والسلام).

وهذا أثار تساؤلات حول ما إذا كانت التقارير عن النبي كان موثوقة وكانت كلماته
محفوظة بدقة مثل كلمات القرآن.

Traditional Muslims believe that Hadith is a very reliable historical source. Secular critical historical scholars strongly dispute this to the point that many reject Hadith narrations because it cannot be reliably traced back to the actual words of the Prophet (May the peace and blessings of Allah be upon him).

This raised the questions on whether the reports of the Prophet were reliable and was his words accurately preserved as that of the Quran.

(سورة الحجر 9-15)

إِنَّا نَحْنُ نَزَّلْنَا ٱلذِّكْرَ وَإِنَّا لَهُ لَحَافِظُونَ

*It is certainly We Who have revealed the Reminder, and **it is certainly We Who will preserve it.***

وأدى هذا أيضًا إلى ظهور حركة في القرن التاسع عشر تسمى "القرآنيون" والتي رفضت مجموعة الأحاديث بأكملها وشككت في سلطة النبي صلى الله عليه وسلم.

وكان اعتقادهم وحجتهم مبنية على أن النبي لم يكن له سلطة إلا أن ينزل القرآن.

THIS ALSO LED TO THE origins of a movement in the nineteenth century called Quranist which rejected the entire Hadith corpus and questioned the authority of the Prophet (May the peace and blessings of Allah be upon him).

Their belief and argument were based on that the Prophet had no authority except to deliver the Quran.

(سورة النحل 16:82)

فإن تولوا فما عليك أيها النبي إلا البلاغ المبين.

*But if they turn away, then **your duty O Prophet is only to deliver the message clearly.***

ويختلف المحدثون السنة ويستشهدون دائمًا بالآية الشهيرة التالية لإثبات أن الأمر ليس كذلك.

THE SUNNI TRADITIONALISTS disagree and always cite the following famous verse to prove that this was not the case.

(سورة النساء 4:59)

يها المؤمنون! أطيعوا الله وأطيعوا الرسول وأولي الأمر منكم. فإن اختلفتم في شيء فردوه إلى الله ورسوله إن كنتم تؤمنون بالله واليوم الآخر. وهذا هو القرار الأفضل والأعدل

O believers! Obey Allah and obey the Messenger and those in authority among you. Should you disagree on anything, then refer it to Allah and His Messenger, if you truly believe in Allah and the Last Day. This is the best and fairest resolution.

الآية أعلاه تنص ضمنا أطيعوا الله وأطيعوا رسول. الكلمة يطيع ولا يكون أمام أولي الأمر منكم. وهذا يعني: «نعم أطيعوا أولي الأمر منكم ما لم يخالف الكتاب وسنة النبي صلى الله عليه وسلم»..."

ثم قال تعالى: "فإن تنازعتم في شيء فردوه إلى الله ورسوله إن كنتم تؤمنون بالله واليوم الآخر". وهذا يشير إلى القرآن والسنة النبوية.

The above verse implicitly states *obey Allah and obey the Messenger*. The word *obey* is not in front of those in authority among you. This implies "Yes obey those in authority among you as long as it does not go against the Quran and Sunnah of the Prophet (May the peace and blessings of Allah be upon him)."

The verse continues "Should you disagree on anything, then refer it to Allah and His Messenger, if you truly believe in Allah and the Last Day." This refers to the Quran and the Sunnah of the Prophet.

(سورة الأحزاب 33:36)

وَمَا كَانَ لِمُؤْمِنٍ وَلَا مُؤْمِنَةٍ إِذَا قَضَى ٱللَّهُ وَرَسُولُهُ أَمْرًا أَن يَكُونَ لَهُمُ ٱلْخِيَرَةُ مِنْ أَمْرِهِمْ ۗ وَمَن يَعْصِ ٱللَّهَ وَرَسُولَهُ فَقَدْ ضَلَّ ضَلَٰلًا مُّبِينًا

It is not for a believing man or woman when Allah and His Messenger decree a matter to have any other choice in that matter. Indeed, whoever disobeys Allah and His Messenger has clearly gone far astray.

فالسنة تتسع للحديث وتقيده. ولا تذكر كتب الحديث ولا تقدم تفاصيل، على سبيل المثال، كيفية أداء الصلاة. في حالة إعطاء جميع كتب الحديث وقراءة عشرات الآلاف من الأحاديث، فلن يعرفوا كيفية أداء الصلاة..

ولا يتم ذلك إلا من خلال السنة التي هي الممارسة الحياتية المعتادة للنبي (عليه الصلاة والسلام) أن المسلمين اليوم يفهمون ويعرفون كيفية الصلاة.

كما تشرح السنة الحج والزكاة والصيام وكيفية تطبيق تعاليم القرآن عمليا في حياتنا اليومية

The Sunnah expands and restricts the Hadith. The books of Hadith do not mention or provide details for example on how to perform Salah. In the event a Revert is given all the books of Hadith and reads tens of thousands of Hadith they will still not know how to perform salah.

It is only through the Sunnah which is the customary prescriptive perpetual living practice of the Prophet (May the peace and blessings of Allah be upon him) that Muslims today understand and know how to pray.

The Sunnah also explains Hajj, Zakat and Fasting as well as how to practically apply the teachings of the Quran in our daily lives.

عن مالك رضي الله عنه :

وصلنا إلى النبي (عليه الصلاة والسلام) وأقام عنده عشرين يوما وليلة. كنا جميعًا صغارًا وفي نفس العمر تقريبًا.

وكان النبي لطيفًا ورحيمًا جدًا. ولما أدرك اشتياقنا إلى عائلاتنا، سأل عن بيوتنا والناس هناك فأخبرناه.

ثم طلب منا أن نرجع إلى أهلنا ونقيم معهم ونعلمهم الدين ونأمرهم بالمعروف. وذكر أيضًا بعض الأشياء الأخرى التي تذكرتها أو نسيتها.

ثم أضاف النبي:صلوا كما رأيتموني أصلي فإذا حضرت الصلاة فليؤذن أحدكم «وليؤمكم أكبركم».

رواه البخاري

Malik (May Allah be pleased with him) narrated:

We came to the Prophet (May the peace and blessings of Allah be upon him) and stayed with him for twenty days and nights. We were all young and of about the same age.

The Prophet was very kind and merciful. When he realized our longing for our families, he asked about our homes and the people there and we told him.

Then he asked us to go back to our families and stay with them and teach them the religion and to order them to do good things. He also mentioned some other things which I have remembered or forgotten.

The Prophet then added, *"Pray as you have seen me praying* and when it is the time for the prayer one of you should pronounce the Adhan and the oldest of you should lead the prayer."

Narrated by Al-Bukhari

حديث الكذب على النبي

Hadith on telling a lie against the Prophet

الأحاديث عموما مليئة بالتناقضات. المشكلة اليوم هي أن غالبية المسلمين يستمعون إلى الأحاديث ويقبلون صحتها.

ومن الأمثلة على ذلك الحديث التالي الذي تم تناقله بشكل جماعي والذي يشمل أصحاب النبي (عليه الصلاة والسلام). واللفظ عمداً ورد في حديث دون الآخر.

ومن المهم أن نلاحظ أن كلا الحديثين من البخاري، وهناك نسختان مختلفتان لنفس الحديث لعلي وأنس، وكلاهما من صحابي النبي..

Hadiths are generally full of contradictions. The problem today is that the majority of Muslims listen to Hadiths and accept it as authentic.

An example is the following Hadith which have been mass transmitted which includes the companions of the Prophet (May the peace and blessings of Allah be upon him). The word intentionally is used in one Hadith and not the other.

It is important to note that both Hadiths are from Al-Bukhari and there are two different versions of the same Hadith by Ali and Anas, both companions of the Prophet.

(روي عن علي (رضي الله عنه) :
النبي (عليه الصلاة والسلام) قال، "لا تكذب علي من أجل من كذب علي فإنه سيدخل النار حتماً".
رواه البخاري

Ali (May Allah be pleased with him) narrated:

The Prophet (May the peace and blessings of Allah be upon him) said, "Do not tell a lie against me for ***whoever tells a lie against me*** then he will surely enter the Hell-fire."

Narrated by Al-Bukhari

عن أنس رضي الله عنه :

إن الذي يمنعني من أن أروي لك عددًا كبيرًا من الأحاديث هو أن النبي (عليه الصلاة والسلام) قال:

«ومن كذب علي متعمدا, ثم ليتبوأ مقعده من النار".

رواه البخاري

Anas (May Allah be pleased with him) narrated:

The fact which stops me from narrating a great number of Hadiths to you is that the Prophet (May the peace and blessings of Allah be upon him) said:

"Whoever tells a lie against me intentionally, then surely let him occupy his seat in Hell-fire."

Narrated by Al-Bukhari

يؤثر الاختلاف في الصياغة بشكل أساسي على فهم ومعنى المعتقدات الدينية. ومن المهم النظر إلى سياق الحديث نفسه ومقارنته بالأحاديث الموازية والتأكد من عدم تعارضه مع آية في القرآن.

The difference in wording fundamentally affects the understanding and meaning of Religious beliefs. It is important to look at the context of the Hadith itself, compare it to parallel Hadiths and ensure it does not contradict a verse in the Quran.

عن عائشة رضي الله عنها :

وكان أبي قد جمع خمسمائة حديث للنبي. وفي الليلة التي فعل فيها ذلك، تقلب في السرير. فقلت: هل بك مرض أو سمعت شيئا؟ وفي الصباح قال: يا ابنتي! ائتني بالأحاديث التي أعطيتك إياها». أحضرتهم. أراد بعض النار وأحرقهم وعندما سألته لماذا أحرقها، قال: "لا أريد أن أموت وهذه الأحاديث معي لأنني وأخشى أن تكون هناك أحاديث ليست في الأصل كما وردت مع أنني سمعتها من أشخاص أثق بهم; أخشى أن أرويهم بهذه الطريقة"

رواه بواسطة *Al-Dhahbiy*

Aisha (May Allah be pleased with her) narrated:

My father had collected five hundred hadiths of the Prophet. On the night he did it, he tossed and turned in bed. I asked, "Do you have an illness or have you heard something?" In the morning, he said, "My daughter! Bring me the hadiths that I gave you." I brought them. He wanted some fire and burned them.

When I asked him why he burned them, he said, "I do not want to die having these hadiths with me because *I am afraid that there are hadiths that are not originally as they are reported though I heard them from people whom I trust*; I am afraid to narrate them that way"
Narratted by *Al-Dhahbiy*

حديث أكل الحوت الميت

Hadith of Eating dead Whale

قد نهى الله في الآية التالية عن أكل لحوم الميتة. وهذه الآية تنطبق على الحيوانات البرية فقط وليس على الكائنات البحرية.

Allah in the following verse forbids eating the decaying flesh of dead animals. This verse applies to land animals only and not sea creatures.

(سورة المائدة 5:3)

حُرِّمَتْ عَلَيْكُمُ ٱلْمَيْتَةُ وَٱلدَّمُ وَلَحْمُ ٱلْخِنزِيرِ وَمَآ أُهِلَّ لِغَيْرِ ٱللَّهِ بِهِۦ وَٱلْمُنْخَنِقَةُ وَٱلْمَوْقُوذَةُ وَٱلْمُتَرَدِّيَةُ وَٱلنَّطِيحَةُ وَمَآ أَكَلَ ٱلسَّبُعُ إِلَّا مَا ذَكَّيْتُمْ وَمَا ذُبِحَ عَلَى ٱلنُّصُبِ وَأَن تَسْتَقْسِمُوا۟ بِٱلْأَزْلَٰمِ ذَٰلِكُمْ فِسْقٌ ٱلْيَوْمَ يَئِسَ ٱلَّذِينَ كَفَرُوا۟ مِن دِينِكُمْ فَلَا تَخْشَوْهُمْ وَٱخْشَوْنِ ٱلْيَوْمَ أَكْمَلْتُ لَكُمْ دِينَكُمْ وَأَتْمَمْتُ عَلَيْكُمْ نِعْمَتِى وَرَضِيتُ لَكُمُ ٱلْإِسْلَٰمَ دِينًا فَمَنِ ٱضْطُرَّ فِى مَخْمَصَةٍ غَيْرَ مُتَجَانِفٍ لِّإِثْمٍ فَإِنَّ ٱللَّهَ غَفُورٌ رَّحِيمٌ

Forbidden to you are carrion, blood, and swine; what is slaughtered in the name of any other than Allah; what is killed by strangling, beating, a fall, or by gored to death; what is partly eaten by a predator being unless you slaughter it; and what is sacrificed on altars.

You are also forbidden to draw lots for decisions. This is all evil. Today the disbelievers have given up all hope of undermining your faith. So, do not fear them; fear Me!

*Today I have perfected your faith for you, completed My favor upon you, and chosen Islam as your way. **But whoever is compelled by extreme hunger not intending to sin** then surely Allah is All-Forgiving, Most Merciful.*

وحديث أكل الحوت الميت يظهر أنه مخالف للقرآن ولكنه في الواقع توضيح لآية: "حرمت عليكم الميتة والدم والخنزير"

The Hadith on eating the dead whale appears that it is contradicting the Quran but is actually clarifying the verse *"Forbidden to you are carrion, blood, and swine."*

(عن أبي عبد الله جابر بن عبد الله (رضي الله عنه):

بعثنا رسول الله صلى الله عليه وسلم لنعترض قافلة لقريش، وولا علينا أبا عبيدة رضي الله عنه. فأعطانا صرة من تمر، فلم يجد لنا غيره.

كان أبو عبيدة يعطينا تمرة. فقيل له: ما كنت تصنع فيه؟ قال: كنا نرضعه كما يرضع الطفل، ثم نشرب بعده ماء يكفينا يوما إلى الليل.

وكنا نضرب ورق الشجر بعصينا ثم ننقعه في الماء ونأكله». وتابع: "ثم اتجهنا نحو ساحل البحر، حيث ظهر لنا ما يشبه الكومة الضخمة. فلما أتيناها وجدنا أنه حيوان يقال له العنبر.

فقال أبو عبيدة: هي ميتة. فقال: لا، بل نحن رسل رسول الله صلى الله عليه وسلم، خرجنا في سبيل الله، والآن اضطررتم فتأكلوا. فلم نزل نأكل منه شهرا حتى سمننا وكنا ثلاثمائة رجل.

ولقد رأيت كيف نستخرج الشحم من تجويف عينه في الأباريق، ثم نقطع منه قطعا مثل الثور أو مثل الثور.

فأخذ منا أبو عبيدة ثلاثة عشر رجلا فأجلسهم في حجرة عينه. فأخذ أحد أضلاعه فثبته، ثم سرج أكبر بعيرنا، فمر من تحت ضلعه.

فأخذنا قطعًا كبيرة من لحمها لتكون مصدرًا للرحلة عودتنا إلى الوطن. فلما قدمنا المدينة أتينا رسول الله صلى الله عليه وسلم فذكرنا له ذلك كله.

فقال: «إنه رزق أخرجه الله لكم، فهل معك من لحمها شيء تطعمنا؟» فأرسلنا إلى رسول الله صلى الله عليه وسلم من لحمها فأكل.

رواه البخاري ومسلم

Abu 'Abdullah Jabir ibn 'Abdullah (May Allah be pleased with him) reported:

The Messenger of Allah (May Allah's peace and blessings be upon him) dispatched us to intercept a caravan belonging to Quraysh, and he appointed Abu Ubaydah (May Allah be pleased with him) as our commander. He gave us a sack of dates as provision, other than which he did not find anything for us.

Abu Ubaydah used to give us one date at a time. He was asked: "What did you use to do with it?" He said: "We used to suck it just as a baby suckles, then we would drink some water after it, which would suffice us for a day until the night.

We also used to beat off tree leaves with our sticks, then soak them in water and eat them." He continued: "We then headed towards the sea coast, where something like a huge mound appeared to us. When we came to it, we found that it was an animal called Al-Anbar (sperm whale).

Abu 'Ubaydah said: "It is a dead animal." Then he said: "No, rather we are the messengers of the Messenger of Allah (May Allah's peace and blessings be upon him) and we have gone out in the cause of Allah. Now you are forced by necessity, so you can eat. We kept on eating from it for a month until we fattened up, and we were three hundred men.

And indeed, I saw how we scooped out fat from the cavity of its eye in pitchers, then we would cut pieces from it like a bull or the size of a bull.Abu Ubaydah took thirteen men from us and seated them in the cavity of its eye. He took one of its ribs and fixed it up, then saddled the largest camel of ours and it passed under it the rib.

We took large pieces of its meat as provision for our journey back home. When we arrived at Madinah, we came to the Messenger of Allah (May Allah's peace and blessings be upon him) and mentioned all of that to him.

There upon, he said: "It is sustenance that Allah brought out for you. Do you have anything from its meat with you, so that you would feed us?" *We sent some of its meat to the Messenger of Allah (May Allah's peace and blessings be upon him) which he ate.*

Narrated by Al-Bukhari as well as Muslim

مزيد من التوضيح موجود في الآية القرآنية ونص الحديث.

Further clarification is found in the following Quranic verse and Hadith text.

(سورة المائدة 5:96)

ويحل لك صيد وأكل المأكولات البحرية ٫متاعاً لكم وللمسافرين. ولكن صيد البر محرم عليكم في الحج. واتقوا الله الذي إليه تحشرون أجمعين

It is lawful for you to hunt and eat seafood, *as a provision for you and for travelers. But hunting on land is forbidden to you while on pilgrimage. Be mindful of Allah to Whom you all will be gathered.*

حديث عن ماء البحر

Hadith on Sea Water

(عن أبي هريرة (رضي الله عنه:
وسئل النبي صلى الله عليه وسلم عن ماء البحر فقال: "ماؤه طاهر، وتحل ميتته"
رواه الترمذي

Abu Huraira (May Allah be pleased with him) reported:
The Prophet, peace and blessings be upon him, was asked about sea water and he said, "Its water is purifying for ablution, *and its dead animals are lawful to eat."*

Narrated by At-Tirmidhi

حديث ماء البحر مكمل ويوضح حديث أكل الحوت الميت. لذلك من المهم دراسة الحديث وفهمه من خلال سياق نصوص الحديث الموازية الأخرى وكذلك القرآن.

The Hadith on sea water complements and explains the Hadith on eating the dead whale. It is therefore important to examine and understand Hadith through the context of other parallel Hadith texts as well as the Quran.

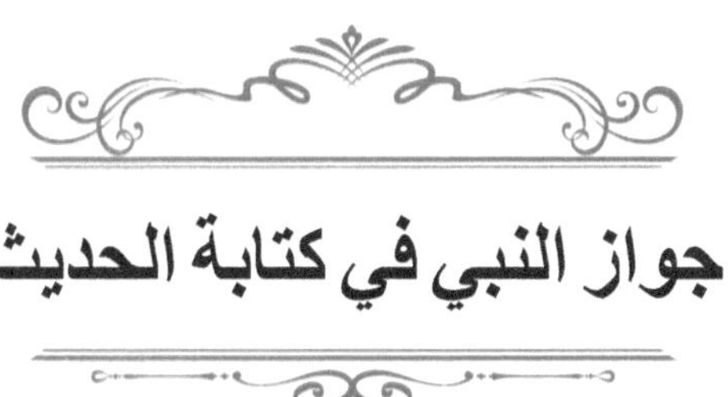

جواز النبي في كتابة الحديث

Prophets Permission to Write down Hadith

النبي (عليه الصلاة والسلام) منع كتابة الحديث أثناء نزول القرآن حتى لا يختلط الحديث بالقرآن. كان التركيز الأساسي في ذلك الوقت هو نزول القرآن وليس الحديث.

The Prophet (May the peace and blessings of Allah be upon him) prohibited the writing of Hadith during the revelation of the Quran to ensure that Hadith doesn't get mixed with the Quran. The main focus at the time was the revelation of the Quran and not Hadith.

عن أبي سعيد الخدري (رضي الله عنه) أن رسول الله (صلى الله عليه وسلم) قال: "لا تكتب عني شيئًا، فمن كتب عني غير القرآن فليمحه، وليحدث عني، فلا بأس بذلك».

رواه مسلم

Abu Said al-Khudri (May Allah be pleased with him) reported that the Messenger of Allah (May the peace and blessings of Allah be upon him) said: "***Do not write anything from me***, whoever has written anything from me other than the Quran, let him erase it and narrate from me, for there is nothing wrong with that."

Narrated by Muslim

وقد تم رفع الحظر بعد نزول القرآن. تم تشجيع تلاوة الحديث الشفهي وتم السماح للناس بكتابة الحديث الذين يخشون أن ينسوا النقل. ال حديث أبي شاه هو مثال على ذلك.

عن أبي هريرة (رضي الله عنه):
وفي عام فتح مكة، قتلت قبيلة خزاعة رجلاً من قبيلة بام الليث انتقاماً لمقتل منهم في الجاهلية.

فقام رسول الله صلى الله عليه وسلم وهو يقول: حبس الله الجيش معه فيلة عن مكة،
وسلط رسوله والمؤمنين على كفار مكة، ألا إن مكة حرم، إن القتال في مكة لا يحل
لأحد. قبلي، ولا يحل لأحد بعدي؛ إلا أحل لي ساعة أو نحوها من ذلك اليوم.
بدون شك! وهو في هذه اللحظة ملاذا. لا ينبغي اقتلاع شجيراتها الشائكة. ولا ينبغي
قطع أشجارها؛ والأشياء الساقطة لا ينبغي أن يلتقطها إلا من يبحث عن صاحبها.
وإذا قُتل إنسان كان لأقرب أقربائه الخيار بين أمرين: إما الدية أو القصاص بقتل
القاتل.» فقام رجل من اليمن يقال له أبو شاه، فقال: "اكتب ذلك ل أنا يا رسول الله
(عليه الصلاة والسلام)"" يا رسول الله قال فقال لأصحابه: اكتبوا لأبي شاه.
فقام رجل آخر من قريش فقال: يا رسول الله! (عليه الصلاة والسلام) إلا الإذخر
فإننا نستعمله في بيوتنا وفي القبور». (عليه الصلاة والسلام) قال: إلا الإذكار
رواه البخاري

THE PROHIBITION WAS lifted after the Quranic revelation. The oral Hadith recitation was encouraged and permission was given to people to write down Hadith who feared they would forget the transmission. The Hadith of Abu Shah is a case in point.

Abu Huraira (May Allah be pleased with him) narrated:

In the year of the Conquest of Mecca, the tribe of Khuza`a killed a man from the tribe of Bam Laith in revenge for a killed person belonging to them in the Pre-lslamic Period of Ignorance.

So, Allah's Apostle got up saying, "Allah held back the army having elephants from Mecca, but He let His Apostle and the believers overpower the infidels of Mecca. Beware! Mecca is a sanctuary! Verily! Fighting in Mecca was not permitted for anybody before me, nor will it be permitted for anybody after me; It was permitted for me only for a while an hour or so of that day.

No doubt! It is at this moment a sanctuary; its thorny shrubs should not be uprooted; its trees should not be cut down; and fallen things should not be picked up except by the one who would look for its owner.

And if somebody is killed, his closest relative has the right to choose one of two things, i.e., either the Blood money or retaliation by having the killer killed." Then a man from Yemen, called Abu Shah, stood up and said, *"Write that for me, O Allah's Messenger (May the peace and blessings of Allah be upon him)!" Allah's Messenger said to his companions, "Write that for Abu Shah."*

Then another man from Quraish got up, saying, "O Allah's Messenger! (May the peace and blessings of Allah be upon him) Except Al- Idhkhir (a special kind of grass) as we use it in our houses and for graves." Allah's Messenger (May the peace and blessings of Allah be upon him) said, "Except Al-idhkkir."

Narrated by Al-Bukhari

(عن عبد الله بن عمرو (رضي الله عنه):
كنت أكتب كل ما سمعته من رسول الله صلى الله عليه وسلم أريد أن أحفظه، فنهاتني قريش عن ذلك.
قالوا: أتكتب كل ما تسمع منه؟ النبي إنسان! ويتكلم وهو غاضب ومسرور». لذلك توقفت عن كتابة الأشياء. فذكرت ذلك للنبي فأشار إلى فيه وقال: "اكتب فوالذي نفسي بيده ما يخرج منه إلا الحق."
رواه أبو داود

Abdullah ibn Amr (May Allah be pleased with him) reported:

I would write down everything I heard from the Messenger of Allah (May the peace and blessings of Allah be upon him) wanting to memorize it, but the Quraysh told me not to do it.

They said, "Do you write down everything you hear from him? The Prophet is a human being! He speaks when he is angry and pleased." So, I stopped writing things down. I mentioned it to the Prophet, and he pointed to his mouth and said, *"Write, for by the One in whose hand is my soul, nothing comes out of it but the truth."*

Narrated by Abu Dawud

حديث عن النبي تكرار العبارة ثلاث مرات

Hadith on Prophet repeating a statement three times

النبي (عليه الصلاة والسلام) كان صبورًا وكان يكرر العبارة ثلاث مرات للتأكد من أن الناس يفهمون معناها.

وكان السبب في ذلك أيضًا هو إعطاء الناس الذين يخافون أن ينسوا كلام النبي وقتًا كافيًا لتدوينه.

(رواه أنس بن مالك (رضي الله عنه).

أن رسول الله صلى الله عليه وسلم كان كرر البيان الثالث مرات حتى يمكن فهمه.

رواه الترمذي

The Prophet (May the peace and blessings of Allah be upon him) was patient and would repeat a statement three times to ensure people understood its meaning.

The reason for this was also to give those people who feared they would forget the Prophets words enough time to write down it down.

Anas bin Malik (May Allah be pleased with him) narrated

that the Messenger of Allah (May the peace and blessing of Allah be upon him) would *repeat a statement three times* so that it could be understood.

Narrated by At-Tirmidhi

حديث الكتابة في الورق

Hadith of writing down on paper

(عن عبيد الله بن عبد الله (رضي الله عنه):

قال ابن عباس: لما مرض النبي (عليه الصلاة و السلام) وقال إن الأمر أصبح أسوأ " ائتوني بصحيفة أكتب لكم كتابا لن تضلوا بعده " فقال عمر: إن النبي قد غلبه الوجع، ومعنا كتاب الله، وحسبنا ذلك». ولكن اختلف أصحاب النبي صلى الله عليه وسلم في ذلك، وكان هناك صيحة وصراخ.

فقال لهم النبي: اذهبوا واتركوني وشأني. ليس من الصواب أن تتشاجروا أمامي فخرج ابن عباس يقول: لقد كان رسول الله صلى الله عليه وسلم شديد الأسف (عليه الصلاة والسلام) فمُنع من كتابة ذلك البيان لهم بسبب اختلافهم وضجيجهم

رواه البخاري

Ubaidullah bin Abdullah (May Allah be pleased with him) narrated:

Ibn 'Abbas said, "When the ailment of the Prophet (May the peace and blessings of Allah be upon him) became worse, he said, *"Bring for me writing paper and I will write for you a statement after which you will not go astray." But Umar said, "The Prophet is seriously ill, and we have got Allah's Book with us and that is sufficient for us."* But the companions of the Prophet differed about this and there was a hue and cry.

On that the Prophet said to them, 'Go away and leave me alone. It is not right that you should quarrel in front of me."

Ibn 'Abbas came out saying, "It was most unfortunate (a great disaster) that Allah's Messenger (May the peace and blessings of Allah be upon him) was prevented from writing that statement for them because of their disagreement and noise.

Narrated by Al-Bukhari

والحديث مفتوح للتأويل فيما يتعلق بما قاله النبي (عليه الصلاة والسلام) أراد أن يكتب قبل وفاته. هل أراد أن يسمي علياً أو عمر أو أحد الصحابة الآخرين خلفاً له أو يؤكد توجيهاته بأن المؤمنين يتبعون القرآن وسنته؟

بيان عمر «إن النبي غلبه الوجع، ومعنا كتاب الله، وحسبنا ذلك». كما يلقي ظلالا من الشك على صحة الحديث كما ولم يكن القرآن قد جمع في ذلك الوقت في شكل كتاب

The Hadith is open to interpretation as to what the Prophet (May the peace and blessings of Allah be upon him) wanted to write down before his death. Did he want to name Ali, Umar or one of the other companions as his successor or reaffirm his instruction that believers follow the Quran and his Sunnah?

Umar's statement ***"The Prophet is seriously ill, and we have got Allah's Book with us and that is sufficient for us."*** also casts a shadow of doubt as to the authenticity of the Hadith as the Quran was not yet at that time compiled in book form.

نقد الحديث

Hadith Criticism

م نقل الحديث في البداية شفهيا ثم مكتوبا في وقت لاحق. وكان عبء توثيق الحديث أصعب لو اقتصر على النقل الشفهي فقط.

والحقيقة هي أن الذاكرة غير موثوقة وإعادة صياغة الحديث يمكن أن تسبب تغييرات في نصها ومعناها الفعلي. كان على المسلمين في ذلك الوقت أن يتحملوا الصراعات القبلية والهجرة الجماعية والتغيرات البيئية التي كان من شأنها أن تؤثر على ذاكرتهم ونقل الحديث الشفهي.

Hadith was initially transmitted orally then later written. The burden to authenticate Hadith would have been harder if it was only confined to oral transmission.

The fact is that memory is unreliable and paraphrasing of Hadith can cause changes in their actual text and meaning. The Muslims at the time had to endure tribal conflicts, mass migration and changes of environment which would have affected their memory and the oral transmissions of Hadith.

قال شعبة بن الحجاج أحد كبار علماء الحديث:

«لا أعلم أحداً من محققي الحديث كان تحقيقه مثل تحقيقي. واكتشفت أن ثلاثة أرباعها كاذبة».

Shu'bah ibn al-Hajjaj who are considered one of the foremost scholars of Hadith criticism said:

"I do not know of anyone who scrutinized Hadith whose investigation was comparable to my investigation. I discovered that three quarters thereof are false."

لم تكن هناك ضوابط مكتوبة عندما تم النقل الشفهي الأولي للحديث. وهذا يتعارض مع القرآن المكتوب حيث يوجد تاريخ قوي من المعرفة والعلم الراسخ. يمكن

للمؤمنين الذين قرأوا القرآن الرجوع دائمًا إلى النص القرآني المكتوب الذي كان شكلاً من أشكال السيطرة.

There were no written controls in place when the initial oral transmission of Hadith took place. This is opposite to the written Quran where a robust history of established background knowledge and scholarship existed. The believers who recited the Quran could always refer back to the written Quranic text which was a form of control.

قال عبد الله بن لهيعة، أحد علماء الحديث المصريين المشهورين: مهرطق تاب إليّ من عقائده الباطلة. هو قال: «انظروا عمن أخذتم هذه الأحاديث، فإنا كلما عقلنا طريقنا إلى مذهب حولناه إلى حديث».

Abdullah ibn Lahi'ah who was a famous Egyptian Hadith Scholar said:

"A heretic who had repented of his false doctrines to me. He said: *"Examine carefully from whom you have taken these Hadith for verily whenever we reasoned our way to a doctrine we would turn it into Hadith."*

ركزت القرون الأربعة الأولى من الحديث الحديث على نقد الإسناد، دون انتقاد محتويات الحديث نفسه.

وقد استخدم البخاري ومسلم وأحمد بن حنبل وآخرون روايات متطابقة في صحة الحديث والتي نجحت إلى حد ما. والسبب في ذلك هو إشكالية الفترة السابقة للحديث حيث لم يكن هناك إسناد لتوثيق الأحاديث.

وهذا يعني أنه منذ القرن الثامن فصاعدًا، كان نقاد الحديث يحاولون تطبيق أساليبهم في توثيق روايات الحديث منذ ما قبل مائة إلى مائة وخمسين عامًا.

The first four centuries of the Hadith tradition were focused on isnad (chain of narrations) criticism which excluded criticizing the contents of the Hadith itself.

Al-Bukhari, Muslim, Ahmad bin Hanbal and others used corroborative transmissions to authenticate Hadith which worked to a certain degree. The reason for this is the problematic earlier period of Hadith as there were no isnads (chain of narrations) in place to authenticate Hadiths.

This means that from the eighth century onwards Hadith critics were trying to *apply their methods to authenticate Hadith narrations from one hundred to one hundred and fifty years earlier.*

وقد ثبت عدم فعاليته بسبب الأسانيد المتوازية الموضوعة للأحاديث في الفترة السابقة. مما يجعل من الصعب التمييز بين الأحاديث الصحيحة والموضوعة تم إنشاء الفجوات في الجدول الزمني الفيل في الغرفة اليوم كلما ذكر أي شخص الحديث. والسبب في ذلك هو أنه عندما يستشهد أي شخص بالحديث، سواء كان في المسجد أو على منصة عامة، سيكون هناك على الأقل شخص واحد أو أكثر من المتشككين الذين سيطرحون السؤال: "هل النبي (حقا يقول صلى الله عليه وسلم ذلك؟

لقد كتب الحديث متأخرا مما يتركه مفتوحا للتأويل بسبب الإسناد المتناقض المتوازي السابق (سلسلة الروايات) للحديث. هذا يجلب الحديث أقرب إلى الشك من (لفظ النبي صلى الله عليه وسلم (عليه الصلاة والسلام.

This proved ineffective due to the fabricated parallel isnads (chain of narrations) for Hadiths in the earlier period making it difficult to distinguish between authentic and fabricated Hadiths.

The gaps in the timeline created the *elephant in the room* today whenever anyone cites Hadith. The reason for this is that when anyone cites Hadith, whether it is in the mosque or on a public platform, there would be at least one or more skeptical persons who would ask the question: *"Did the Prophet (May the peace and blessings of Allah be upon him) really actually say that?"*

Hadith was written late which leaves it open to interpretation due to the earlier parallel contradictory isnads (chain of narrations) for Hadith. This brings *Hadith closer to the realm of skepticism than the literal words of the Prophet (May the peace and blessings of Allah be upon him).*

الحديث ضرورة لأنه يزودنا بمعلومات عن السنة النبوية (عليه الصلاة والسلام) ويوفر السياق للآيات القرآنية. كما أنه يزودنا برؤية ثاقبة لآراء وآراء الأجيال السابقة من المسلمين.

الطوائف الإسلامية مثل السنة والشيعة والسلفية والصوفية والوهابية وغيرها كلها تقبل الحديث ضروري لفهم القرآن والسنة النبوية (عليه الصلاة والسلام) على الرغم من أنه قد يكون لديهم خلافات عندما يتعلق الأمر بالحديث.
المسلمون، رغم اختلافهم في التأويل والفهم، يتمسكون بالعقيدة يحظى القرآن والحديث بتقدير كبير كمصدر إرشادي لمعتقداتهم الدينية.

Hadith is a necessity as it provides us with information on the Sunnah of the Prophet (May the peace and blessings of Allah be upon him) and provides context to Quranic verses. It also provides us with insight on the views and opinions of the earlier generations of Muslims.

Muslim sects like Sunni, Shia, Salafi, Sufi, Wahabi etc all accept Hadith is necessary to understand the Quran and the Sunnah of the Prophet (May the peace and blessings of Allah be upon him) even though they might have disagreements when it comes to Hadith.

Muslims, despite their differences in interpretations and understanding, hold the ***Quran and Hadith in high esteem as a source of guidance for their religious beliefs.***

الفصل الثاني
الفرق بين القرآن والحديث

CHAPTER TWO
Differences between the Quran and Hadith

(سورة العنكبوت 29:45)

ٱتْلُ مَآ أُوحِىَ إِلَيْكَ مِنَ ٱلْكِتَـٰبِ وَأَقِمِ ٱلصَّلَوٰةَ ۖ إِنَّ ٱلصَّلَوٰةَ تَنْهَىٰ عَنِ ٱلْفَحْشَآءِ وَٱلْمُنكَرِ ۗ وَلَذِكْرُ ٱللَّهِ أَكْبَرُ ۗ وَٱللَّهُ يَعْلَمُ مَا تَصْنَعُونَ

Recite what has been revealed to you of the Book and establish prayer.

القرآن يقرأ في كل صلاة والحديث لا يقرأ في الصلاة.

The Quran is recited in every prayer while Hadith cannot be recited in prayer

(Surah Al-Isra 17:88)

قل يا أيها النبي لو اجتمعت الإنس والجن على أن يأتوا بمثل هذا القرآن لا يأتون بمثله مهما ظفروا.

Say, O Prophet, "If all humans and jinn were to come together to produce the equivalent of this Quran, they could not produce its equal, no matter how they supported.

القرآن يحتوي على كلام الله المطهّر غير المحرف بينما الحديث منسوب إلى أقوال النبي وأفعاله ﷺ

The Quran contains the pure unaltered words of Allah while Hadith is attributed to words and actions of the Prophet ﷺ

(Surah An-Najm 53:2-4)

ما ضل صاحبكم (محمد) ولم يخطئ. ولا يتكلم عن هواه. إن هو إلا وحي يوحي.

Your companion (Muhammad) has neither gone astray nor has erred. Nor does he speak from his own inclination. It is not but a revelation revealed.

لقد جاء القرآن إلى النبي محمد عن طريق الملاك جبريل، في حين أن الحديث عبارة عن روايات عن حياة النبي من مصادر مثل البخاري ومسلم وغيرهما.

The Quran has been brought to the Prophet Muhammad by the Angel Gabriel, while Hadith are narrations about the Prophet's life from sources like Bukhari, Muslim and others.

(سورة فاطر 35: 29-30)

إِنَّ ٱلَّذِينَ يَتْلُونَ كِتَـٰبَ ٱللَّهِ وَأَقَامُوا ٱلصَّلَوٰةَ وَأَنفَقُوا مِمَّا رَزَقْنَـٰهُمْ سِرًّا وَعَلَانِيَةً يَرْجُونَ تِجَـٰرَةً لَّن تَبُورَ لِيُوَفِّيَهُمْ أُجُورَهُمْ وَيَزِيدَهُم مِّن فَضْلِهِ إِنَّهُ غَفُورٌ شَكُورٌ

Surely those who recite the Book of Allah, establish prayer, and donate from what We have provided for them—secretly and openly—can hope for an exchange that will never fail. so that **He will reward them in full and increase them out of His grace.** He is truly All-Forgiving, Most Appreciative.

إن تلاوة القرآن لها ثواب وفضائل، وتلاوة الحديث وسيلة من وسائل البركة.

((بركاته

The recitation of the Quran has measured rewards and virtues while the recitation of Hadith is a means of barakah. (blessings)

(سورة البقرة 2:106)

ما ننسخ من آية أو ننسها نبدلها بخير منها أو مثلها. ألا تعلم أن الله على كل شيء قدير؟

If We ever abrogate a verse or cause it to be forgotten, We replace it with a better or similar one. Do you not know that Allah is Most Capable of everything?

القرآن معجزة وفريدة من نوعها. الحديث ليس على نفس المستوى من العجب والرهبة. الحديث لا يمكن أن ينسخ آية من القرآن.

The Quran is a miracle and unique. Hadith does not have the same level of wonder and awe. Hadith can never abrogate a verse of the Quran.

(Surah Al-Waqi'ah 56:74-79)

فَسَبِّحْ بِٱسْمِ رَبِّكَ ٱلْعَظِيمِ فَلَا أُقْسِمُ بِمَوَٰقِعِ ٱلنُّجُومِ وَإِنَّهُ لَقَسَمٌ لَّوْ تَعْلَمُونَ عَظِيمٌ إِنَّهُ لَقُرْءَانٌ كَرِيمٌ فِى كِتَـٰبٍ مَّكْنُونٍ لَّا يَمَسُّهُ إِلَّا ٱلْمُطَهَّرُونَ

*So, glorify the Name of your Lord, the Greatest. So, I do swear by the positions of the stars—and this, if only you knew, is **indeed a great oath that this is truly a noble Quran, in a well-preserved Record touched by none except the purified angels.***

لا يجوز مس القرآن على غير وضوء أو على جنابة. يجوز مس كتب الحديث على جنابة وبدون وضوء.

The Quran cannot be touched without wudu or in a state of sexual impurity. The books of Hadith can be touched in a state of sexual impurity and without wudu.

(سورة يوسف 2:12)

إِنَّآ أَنزَلْنَهُ قُرْءَٰنًا عَرَبِيًّا لَّعَلَّكُمْ تَعْقِلُونَ

*Indeed, **We have sent it down as an Arabic Quran** so that you may understand.*

.ولا يجوز قراءة القرآن بلغته إلا العربية، بينما يجوز رواية الحديث بأي لغة

The Quran cannot be recited in one's own language except Arabic while Hadith may be narrated in any language.

(سورة العنكبوت 29:47)

وَمَا يَجْحَدُ بِـَٔايَٰتِنَآ إِلَّا ٱلْكَٰفِرُونَ

And none denies Our revelations except the stubborn disbelievers.

يمكنك أن تفقد إيمانك برفض آية من القرآن. وليس هذا إذا كنت ترفض رواية الحديث.

You can lose your Iman (faith) by rejecting a verse of the Quran. This is not the case if you reject a Hadith narration.

(سورة الحجر 15:9)

إِنَّا نَحْنُ نَزَّلْنَا ٱلذِّكْرَ وَإِنَّا لَهُ لَحَٰفِظُونَ

It is certainly We Who have revealed the Reminder, and it is certainly We Who will preserve it.

القرآن لا مثيل له وحفظه الله من أي تحريف. الحديث ليس محفوظا مثل القرآن ومليء بالتناقضات.

The Quran is incomparable and protected by Allah against any corruption. Hadith is not preserved like the Quran and is full of contradictions.

الفصل الثالث
القرآن في ضوء الحديث

CHAPTER THREE
The Quran in light of the Hadith

(سورة آل عمران 3:31)

قل يا أيها النبي إن كنتم تحبون الله صادقين فاتبعوني ؛الله يحبك ويغفر ذنوبك. إن الله غفور رحيم».

Say, O Prophet, "If you sincerely love Allah, then follow me; Allah will love you and forgive your sins. For Allah is All-Forgiving, Most Merciful."

القرآن وحي إلهي مكتوب من الله بينما الحديث كان خاضعًا للنقل الشفهي ثم النقل المكتوب لاحقًا المنسوب إلى رسول الله. (عليه الصلاة والسلام

The Quran is divine written revelation from Allah while Hadith was subject to oral transmission and then later written transmission attributed to the Messenger of Allah. (May the blessings and peace of Allah be upon him)

(سورة عبس 80: 11-14)

لكن لا! وهذا الوحي هو حقا تذكير. فليتذكر ذلك من شاء. وهو مكتوب على الصفحات التي عقدت على شرف ـمحترم جدًا، مطهر.

*But no! This revelation is truly a reminder. So, let whoever wills be mindful of it. **It is written on pages held in honor**—highly esteemed, purified.*

القرآن يبين كل شيء وهو بذرة كل علم. السنة النبوية توسع القرآن وتقيده.

والسبب في ذلك هو أن السنة توفر سياقًا لآيات القرآن وهي أيضًا عدسة لكيفية قراءة القرآن وفهمه. وفي حالة اختلاف المسلمين في تفسير آية قرآنية فإن السنة تحدد حدود هذا التفسير.

The Quran elucidates all things and is the seed of all knowledge. The Sunnah of the Prophet expands and restricts the Quran.

The reason for this is that the Sunnah provides context to the verses of the Quran and is also the lens on how we read and understand the Quran. In the event Muslims differ on the interpretation of a Quranic verse the Sunnah restricts the boundaries of such interpretation

(سورة البقرة 2:2)

هذا هو الكتاب! لا شك في هذا ـ هدى للمتقين في الله.

*This is the Book! There is no doubt about it—**a guide for those mindful of Allah.***

»فقال رسول الله صلى الله عليه وسلم: »إني أوتيت القرآن ومثله معه.

عن المقدام بن معديكرب قال: قال رسول الله صلى الله عليه وسلم: »لقد أوتيت القرآن ومثله معه. وسيأتي زمان الرجل متكئ على أريكته يقول: إنما اتبعوا القرآن، وأحلوا ما وجدتم فيه حلالا، وحرموا ما وجدتم فيه من حرام.

رواه أبو داود

The Messenger of Allah (May the blessings and peace of Allah be upon him) said "I have been given the Quran and something similar along with it."

Al-Miqdam ibn Ma'dikarib reported: The Messenger of Allah, peace and blessings be upon him, said, *"I have surely been given the Quran and something similar along with it.* Soon, the time will come when a man will recline on his couch, saying: "Only follow the Quran, make lawful what you find in it as lawful and outlaw what you find in it as unlawful."

Narrated by Abu Dawud

(سورة الحشر 59:7)

وما آتاكم الرسول فخذوه. وما نهاكم عنه فانتركوه. واتقوا الله.

Whatever the Messenger gives you, take it. And whatever he forbids you from, leave it. And fear Allah.

القرآن يوافق السنة ويشرح الحديث.

وتشير التقديرات إلى أن ثمانين بالمائة من الشريعة الإسلامية مستمدة من الحديث وليس من القرآن. هناك عشرات الآلاف من الأحاديث التي معظمها له آثار قانونية مقارنة بالأحكام الشرعية القليلة في القرآن.

وقد خلق هذا تصورًا بين الأمة بأن الحديث هو كلام الله الحرفي. ليس هناك مقارنة أو مساواة مع الله و هذا يشمل كلامه.

The Quran approves the Sunnah and explains the Hadith.

It is estimated that eighty percent of Islamic law is derived from Hadith and not Quran. There are tens of thousands of Hadiths of which most have legal implications in comparison to the Qurans few legal provisions.

This has created the perception amongst the Ummah that Hadith is the verbatim words of Allah. There is no comparison or equal to Allah and this includes His words.

(سورة طه 20:14)

إِنَّنِىٓ أَنَا ٱللَّهُ لَآ إِلَٰهَ إِلَّآ أَنَا فَٱعْبُدْنِى وَأَقِمِ ٱلصَّلَوٰةَ لِذِكْرِىٓ

It is truly I. I am Allah! There is no god worthy of worship except Me. So, worship Me alone, and establish prayer for My remembrance

يجب أن يكون هناك إعادة التوازن بين القرآن والحديث. يجب استعادة المنظور القرآني حيث أن تقليد الحديث قد تجاوز القرآن.

دستور المملكة العربية السعودية هو القرآن. لا يوجد قانون جزائي أو مدني، ويصدر القضاة أحكامهم بناءً على الشريعة الإسلامية.

There needs to be a restoration of balance between the Quran and Hadith. The Quranic perspective needs to be restored as the tradition of Hadith has overtaken the Quran.

The constitution of Saudi Arabia is the Quran. There is no penal or civil code and judges make rulings based on the Shariah (Islamic law)

ولي العهد السعودي، (MBS) في مقابلة مع قناة العربية, قال محمد بن سلمان: "الحكومة التي تهتم بالشريعة لديها لتطبيق أحكام القرآن وتعاليمه في الحديث المتواتر (المعروف).والنظر في صحة أحاديث الآحاد ومصداقيتها وترك أحاديثأخبار جملة وتفصيلا إلا إذا كان فيها منفعة واضحة للإنسانية

لذلك، ينبغي أن يكون هناك ولا عقوبة في الدين إلا بنص قرآني وا الضح، وينفذ هذا الحد على ما فعله النبي صلى الله عليه وسلم.

ويترتب على ذلك أن تختفي بعض القوانين الإسلامية مثل قتل المرتد والشواذ والرجم وقطع أيدي السارق.

وهذا يعني ذلك أيضًا ولن يبقى سوى عشرة بالمائة من الأحاديث الصحيحة المتوافقة مع النص القرآني في مكانها.

ال التحول في الأيديولوجية أماكن التركيز بشكل أقوى على القرآن و أ رفض الأحاديث إذا لم تكن مدعمة بآية قرآنية.

In an interview with Al-Arabiya, Mohammed Bin Salman (MBS), the Crown Prince of Saudi Arabia said:

"The government where Sharia is concerned has to *implement Quran regulations and teachings in a mutawtir (well known) hadith,* and to look into the veracity and reliability of Ahad (isolated) hadiths and to disregard khabar (hearsay) hadiths entirely unless if a clear benefit is derived from it for humanity."

So, there should be *no punishment related to a religious matter except when there is a clear Quranic stipulation,* and this penalty will be implemented based on the way that the Prophet applied it."

The implications are that some Islamic laws would disappear such as the death of the apostate and homosexuals, stoning and amputating the hands of thieves.

This also means that only *ten percent of valid Hadith which are aligned to the Quranic text will remain in place.*

The *shift in ideology* places *stronger emphasis on the Quran* and a *rejection of Hadiths if it is not collaborated with by a Quranic verse.*

يقرأ المسلمون القرآن بشكل عام دون فهم و غالباً ما يخلطون بين آيات القرآن ونصوص الحديث.

تعتمد الشريعة الإسلامية في الغالب على تعليمات مفصلة من نصوص الحديث.

يحتوي القرآن على أوامر عامة بينما يقدم الحديث تفاصيل محددة بخصوص الآيات القرآنية.

الآيات القرآنية المتعلقة بالصلاة والصيام والحج والزكاة والمعاملات التجارية تحتاج إلى توضيح. النبي (عليه الصلاة والسلام) وبينت آيات القرآن عمليا والتي يعتبرها كثير من المسلمين اليوم وحيا آخر يسمى السنة. الحديث يتوسع في النصوص القرآنية عندما يتعلق الأمر بالصلاة والحج والصيام وما إلى ذلك. ونصوص الحديث مقارنة بالنصوص القرآنية واسعة جدًا.

Muslims generally recite the Quran without understanding and often *confuse verses of the Quran with the texts of Hadith.*

Islamic law is mostly based on detailed instruction from Hadith texts. The Quran has general commands while Hadith provides specific details regarding Quranic verses.

The Quran verses regarding prayer, fasting, Hajj, Zakah and commercial transactions required clarification. The Prophet (May the peace and blessing of Allah be upon him) demonstrated the verses of the Quran practically which many Muslims today consider another revelation called the Sunnah.

The *Hadith expands on the Quranic texts* when it comes to prayer, Hajj, Fasting etc. The texts of Hadith in comparison to the Quranic texts are very vast.

(سورة يوسف 12:108)

قلأيها يا النبي هذه سبيلي. أخبرهم أن هذا هو طريقي الواضح والمستقيم. إن دعوتي مبنية على قناعة راسخة وعقل ومعرفة وفهم – لي وكذلك لأتباعي

*Say, O Prophet, "This is my way. Tell them that this is my way which is very clear and straight. **My call is based on firm conviction, reason, knowledge, and understanding** – mine as well as that of my followers.*

كلمات القرآن والحديث لها معنى. تفسيرنا للكلمات مهم لأنه يشكل واقعنا فيما يتعلق بالأهمية السياقية للنصوص القرآنية والحديثية

إن تفكيرنا من خلال المعرفة والفهم الأساسيين سيخبرنا أن القرآن هو المصدر الرئيسي للوحي الإلهي.

ويجب اتباع وصايا الله. القرآن الذي هو كلام الله المختصر والدقيق يحكم السنة. لن يكون هناك نبي (عليه الصلاة والسلام) أو الوحي الإلهي بدون القرآن.

The words of the Quran and Hadith have meaning. Our interpretation of words matters as it shapes our reality as to the contextual importance of Quranic and Hadith texts.

Our reasoning through established background knowledge and understanding will inform us that the Qur'an is the main source of divine revelation.

The commandments of Allah must be followed. The Quran which is the concise and precise words of Allah rules over the Sunnah. There would be no Prophet (May the peace and blessing of Allah be upon him) or divine revelation without the Quran.

(سورة علي عمران 3:7)

هو الذي أنزل عليك أيها النبي الكتاب ٬وفيه بعض الآيات دقيقة۔ هم أم الكتاب ـ والبعض الآخر بعيد المنال.

ويتبع أصحاب القلوب المنحرفة هذه الآيات المراوغة سعيًا إلى إثارة الشك من خلال تفسيراتها الباطلة، ولكن لا أحد يدرك معناها الكامل إلا الله. وأما الراسخون في العلم فيقولون آمنا بهذا القرآن كل من عند ربنا. ولكن لا يراعي ذلك إلا أهل العقل.

*He is the One Who has revealed to you O Prophet the Book, **of which some verses are precise**—they the foundation of the Book—while are others are elusive*

*Those with deviant hearts follow the elusive verses seeking to spread doubt through their false interpretations—but none grasps their full meaning except Allah. As for those well-grounded in knowledge, they say, "We believe in this Quran—it is all from our Lord." **But none will be mindful of this except people of reason.***

يبتلي الله الناس بالآيات المراوغة، وذوي القلوب المنحرفة سيشككون في القرآن من خلال تأويلاتهم الباطلة.

وهذا يسبب ارتباكًا بين الأمة الذين يلجأون إلى الحديث باعتباره المصدر الرئيسي للمعرفة والإرشاد. وتجميع الحديث وتوثيقه موجود منذ ألف وأربعمائة سنة الأحاديث المليئة بالتناقضات بشكل عام تخضع للتفسيرات اليوم على الرغم من أن الكثيرين ينظرون إلى الحديث باعتباره المصدر الرئيسي للشريعة الإسلامية.

وهذا لا يعني أن الحديث يجب رفضه تماما. وينبغي أن يكون الإجماع على أنه لا ينبغي النظر إلى الحديث بمعزل عن غيره.

Allah tests people with elusive verses and those with deviant hearts will spread doubt about the Quran through their false interpretations.

This causes confusion amongst the Ummah who turn to Hadith as the main source of knowledge and guidance. The compilation and authentication of Hadith have been in existence for the last fourteen hundred years.

Hadiths which are generally full of contradictions are subject to interpretations today even though many view Hadith as the main source of Islamic law.

This does not mean that Hadith should be totally rejected. The consensus should be that Hadith should not be viewed in isolation.

كثيرا ما يطرح السؤال "ماذا لو لم يذكر القرآن حديثا يعتبر صحيحا؟" ينبغي فحص الحديث في محاولة لفهم سياقه ومقارنته بالأحاديث الموازية الأخرى.
السبب في ذلك هو ذلك لكل الحديث الصحيح من المحتمل أن يكون هناك حديث آخر مواز ومعاكس له وهو غير صحيح. وهذا صحيح بغض النظر عما إذا كان مصدر المعلومات من البخاري أو مسلم أو غيرهما.

The question often arises *"What if the Quran doesn't mention a Hadith that is considered authentic?"* The Hadith in an effort to understand its context should be examined and compared to other parallel Hadiths.

The reason for this is that *for every Hadith that is true there is potentially another equally parallel and opposite Hadith that is untrue.* This holds true irrespective if the source of information is from Bukhari, Muslim or others.

العلماء الغربيون بما فيهم المسلمون يشككون بشكل عام في الحديث وعادة ما يطبقون المنهج النقدي التاريخي عند التعامل مع الحديث.
تتضمن هذه الطريقة فحص أصول نص الحديث التاريخي والتحقيق في مصادره وتاريخه والأحداث التي كتب فيها النص، وكذلك الأشخاص والأماكن والعادات والأشياء التي وردت في النص.

إن اتباع مثال عملي لحياة النبي أسهل من اتباع النصوص القرآنية وتفسيرها.
والمشكلة أيضًا هي أن اللغة العربية ليست اللغة الأولى لمعظم المسلمين في كثير
من الأحيان صعب الفهم.

وكان وضوح القرآن أوضح عند الصحابة في خطهم الزمني حيث نزل القرآن
بلغتهم ولهجتهم.

Western scholars including Muslims are generally skeptical about Hadith and usually apply the historical critical method when dealing with Hadith.

This method involves examining the historical Hadith text origins and investigates its sources, the date, events in which the text was written, as well as persons, places, customs and things that are mentioned in the text.

It is easier to follow a practical example of the Prophet's life than to follow and interpret Quranic texts. An issue also is that Arabic is not most Muslims first language making it often times difficult to understand.

The clarity of the Quran was clearer to the Sahabah in their timeline as the Quran was revealed in their language and dialect.

(سورة يوسف 2:12)

إِنَّآ أَنزَلْنَـٰهُ قُرْءَٰنًا عَرَبِيًّا لَّعَلَّكُمْ تَعْقِلُونَ

*Indeed, We have sent it down as an **Arabic Quranso that you may understand***

وهذا يعني أيضاً أن النبي (عليه الصلاة والسلام) وأوضح المعاني العميقة للآيات
التي لم ترد في القرآن.

يحتاج غالبية المسلمين اليوم إلى مترجم لفهم القرآن الكريم. ويمكن للعلماء مثل
الأئمة والمشايخ تقديم الدعم في هذا الصدد ولكن في نطاق محدود بسبب ضيق
الوقت.

يعتبر الوقت ترفًا في حياتنا المزدحمة سريعة الخطى. لدينا التزامات عائلية وعملية
واجتماعية ودينية. أين نجد الوقت لتعلم القرآن وفهمه؟

This also implies that the Prophet (May the peace and blessing of Allah be upon him) explained the deeper meanings of the verses that were not mentioned in the Quran.

The majority of Muslims today need an interpreter to understand the Quran. The scholars like the Imams and Sheikhs can provide support in this regard but to a limited extent due to time constraints.

Time is considered a luxury in our busy fast paced lives. We have family, work, social and religious commitments. Where do we find time to learn and understand the Quran?

(Surah Al-Isra 17:106)

إنه قرآن أنزلناه على مراحل لكي تكونوا يمكن قراءتها للناس بوتيرة متعمدة. وأنزلناه آيات متتابعة.

*It is a Quran We have revealed in stages so that you **may recite it to people at a deliberate pace.** And We have sent it down in successive revelations*

لقد قدم العصر الرقمي للتعلم فرصة لأي شخص للمشاركة بنشاط وتعلم القرآن باستخدام التقنيات والموارد الرقمية عبر الإنترنت عبر أجهزة الكمبيوتر المكتبية وأجهزة التلفزيون iPad والكمبيوتر المحمول والكمبيوتر اللوحي والهواتف الذكية الذكية وغيرها.

هناك تطبيقات إسلامية مجانية اليوم تربط المستخدمين بالقرآن، وتحسن تلاوتهم وحفظهم للقرآن مع بناء عادات إيجابية في هذه العملية.

The digital age of learning has presented an opportunity for anyone to actively engage and learn the Quran using digital technologies and resources online via their desktop, laptop, tablet, iPad smartphone, smart TV's and others.

There are free Muslim apps today that connect users with the Quran, improve their recitation and memorization of the Quran while building positive habits in the process.

(سورة التوبة 9:31)

ٱتَّخَذُوٓاْ أَحْبَارَهُمْ وَرُهْبَٰنَهُمْ أَرْبَابًا مِّن دُونِ ٱللَّهِ وَٱلْمَسِيحَ ٱبْنَ مَرْيَمَ وَمَآ أُمِرُوٓاْ إِلَّا لِيَعْبُدُوٓاْ إِلَٰهًا وَٰحِدًا ۖ لَّآ إِلَٰهَ إِلَّا هُوَ ۚ سُبْحَٰنَهُۥ عَمَّا يُشْرِكُونَ

They have taken their rabbis and monks as well as the Messiah, son of Mary, as lords besides Allah, even though they were commanded to worship none but One God. There is no god worthy of worship except Him. Glorified is He above what they associate with Him!

النبي (عليه الصلاة والسلام) كما يحذرنا من الاستماع إلى العلماء الذين تعاليمها مخالفه للقرآن.

عدي بن حاتم (رضي الله عنه) قال:

سمعت النبي صلى الله عليه وسلم يقرأ هذه الآية: "لقد اتخذوا علمائهم والرهبان أرباب من دون الله والمسيح ابن مريم "

وما أمروا إلا ليعبدوا إلهاً واحداً. لا إله إلا هو. تعالى عما يشركون به.

فقلت له: لا نعبدهم. رد: "أليس يحرمون ما أحل الله فتحرمونه؟ أليس يحلون ما حرم الله فتحلونه؟"" قلت نعم. هو قال: »هكذا تعبدونهم«.

رواه الترمذي

The Prophet (May the peace and blessing of Allah be upon him) also ***warns us not to listen to scholars whose teachings are against the Quran.***

Adiyy ibn Hātim (May Allah be pleased with him) reported:

I heard the Prophet (May the peace and blessings of Allah be upon him) recite this verse: "***They have taken their scholars and monks as lords besides Allah, and also the Messiah, the son of Mariyam.***"

And they were not commanded except to worship one God; there is no deity except Him. Exalted is He above whatever they associate with Him.

So, I said to him: "We do not worship them." He replied: ***"Don't they forbid what Allah allows, so you forbid it? Don't they allow what Allah forbids, so you allow it?"*** I said: Yes. He said: ***"That is how you worship them."***

Narrated by At-Tirmidhi

يهدي الله من يحاول قراءة القرآن وفهمه إلى طريقه.

Allah guides whoever attempts to read and understand the Quran towards His path.

(سورة ص 38:29)

هذا كتاب مبارك أنزلناه إليك أيها النبي لعلهم وتدبروا آياته ولعل أولي العقل يعقلون.

*This is a blessed Book which We have revealed to you O Prophet so that they may **contemplate its verses, and people of reason may be mindful.***

أفضل طريقة لتفسير القرآن هي من خلال القرآن نفسه ونصوص الحديث. يجب ألا يتعارض نص الحديث مع آية من القرآن، أو يتعارض مع العلم والعقل والمنطق والفطرة السليمة. فالآية القرآنية المفسرة المقصودة نفسها، والآيات الخمس الأولى قبلها والآيات الخمس التي بعدها تحتاج إلى دراسة لفهم السياق الكامل للآية. سيوفر هذا سياق عمل عملي عند مقارنة الآيات القرآنية بنصوص الحديث والعكس.

ويستند هذا إلى منطق سليم مفاده أنه من أجل فهم شيء ما بشكل صحيح، يحتاج المرء إلى وضع الأشياء المتقاربة أو المتشابهة معًا.

The best way to interpret the Quran is through the Quran itself and Hadith texts.

Hadith text must not contradict a verse of the Quran, or go against science, reason, logic and common sense. The intended interpreted Quranic verse itself, the first five verses before and the five verses after needs to be examined to understand the full context of the verse. This will provide a practical working context when comparing Quranic verses with Hadith texts and vice versa.

This is based on sound reasoning that in order to make proper sense of something one needs to put things that are close or similar together.

(Surah An-Najm 53:3-4)

ولا يتكلم عن أهوائه .إن هو إلا وحي نزل عليه

Nor does he speak of his own whims. It is only a revelation sent down to him..

لقد نزل الوحي الإلهي على رسول الله (صلى الله عليه وسلم) في وقت واجه فيه النبي وأمته صعوبة واضطهادا شديدين.

يوفر الحديث سياقًا مهمًا في فهم الأحداث التي أدت إلى نزول الآيات القرآنية. ويشمل ذلك أيضًا تأمل القرآن ويقدم نظرة ثاقبة للمسلمين اليوم حول كيفية التغلب على التجارب والمحن.

The divine revelation was revealed to the Messenger of Allah (May the blessings and peace of Allah be upon him) at a time when the Prophet and his Ummah faced great difficulty and persecution.

Hadith provides an important context in understanding the events that led to the revelation of Quranic verses. This also includes the contemplation of the Quran and provides insight for Muslims today on how to overcome trials and tribulations

(سورة سبأ 34:46)

تَتَفَكَّرُوا ۚ قُلْ إِنَّمَا أَعِظُكُم بِوَٰحِدَةٍ ۖ أَن تَقُومُوا لِلَّهِ مَثْنَىٰ وَفُرَٰدَىٰ ثُمَّ تَتَفَكَّرُوا

*Say, O Prophet, "I advise you to do only one thing: stand up for the sake of Allah individually or in pairs—**then reflect.***

القرآن كلام الله وليس كلام رسول الله صلى الله عليه وسلم

The Quran is the words of Allah and not the words of the Messenger of Allah (May the blessings and peace of Allah be upon him)

(Surah An-Nahl 16:82)

ولكن إذا انصرفوا، ثم ما عليك أيها النبي إلا البلاغ الواضح.

*But if they turn away, then **your duty O Prophet is only to deliver the message clearly.***

وكان رسول الله (صلى الله عليه وسلم) أ قرآن يمشي وأكمل مثال يحتذى به البشر لإحياء القرآن.

وعن قتادة رضي الله عنه:

فقلت لعائشة: يا أم المؤمنين أخبريني عن خلق رسول الله صلى الله عليه وسلم.

فقالت عائشة: أما قرأت القرآن؟ فقلت: «يا بالطبع». فقالت عائشة: حقا. "كان خلق رسول الله صلى الله عليه وسلم القرآن".

رواه مسلم

The Messenger of Allah (May the blessings and peace of Allah be upon him) was a ***walking Quran*** and the most perfect excellent example for mankind to follow to bring the Quran to life.

Qatadah (May Allah be pleased with him) reported:

I said to Aisha, "O mother of the believers, tell me about the character of the Messenger of Allah (May the peace and blessings of Allah be upon him)."

Aisha said, "Have you not read the Quran?" I said, "Of course." Aisha said, "***Verily, the character of the Prophet of Allah was the Quran.***"
Narrated by Muslim

إن الحديث في سياق حياة رسول الله صلى الله عليه وسلم يفتح لنا نافذة لنرى كيف كان يطبق الآيات القرآنية عمليا في الحياة اليومية.

The Hadith in the context of the Seerah of the Messenger of Allah (May the blessings and peace of Allah be upon him) life opens a window for us to view how he practically applied the Quranic verses in daily life.

(Surah Al-Ahzab 33:21)

لَّقَدْ كَانَ لَكُمْ فِى رَسُولِ ٱللَّهِ أُسْوَةٌ حَسَنَةٌ لِّمَن كَانَ يَرْجُوا ٱللَّهَ وَٱلْيَوْمَ ٱلْءَاخِرَ وَذَكَرَ ٱللَّهَ كَثِيرًا

Indeed, *in the Messenger of Allah you have an excellent example* for whoever has hope in Allah and the Last Day, and remembers Allah often.

(في رسول (سورة البقرة 2:269

يُؤْتِى ٱلْحِكْمَةَ مَن يَشَاءُ ۚ وَمَن يُؤْتَ ٱلْحِكْمَةَ فَقَدْ أُوتِىَ خَيْرًا كَثِيرًا ۗ وَمَا يَذَّكَّرُ إِلَّا أُولُوا ٱلْأَلْبَـٰبِ

He grants wisdom to whoever He wills. And whoever is granted wisdom is certainly blessed with a great privilege. *But none will be mindful of this except people of reason.*

:عن جندب بن عبد الله (رضي الله عنه) قال

رسول الله (عليه الصلاة والسلام) قال, «اقرأوا القرآن ودرسوه ما اتفقتم في تفسيره ومعانيه, ولكن عندما يكون هناك اختلاف في تفسيره ومعانيه، فعليك التوقف عن تلاوته في الوقت الحالي.

رواه البخاري

Jundab bin Abdullah (May Allah be pleased with him) narrated:

Allah's Messenger (May the peace and blessing of Allah be upon him) said, *"Recite and study the Qur'an as long as you agree as to its interpretation and meanings*, but when you have differences regarding its interpretation and meanings, then you should stop reciting it for the time being.

Narrated by Al-Bukhari

يفتح الله الطريق إلى المعرفة عندما نبدأ باستخدام العقل عند قراءة القرآن، وهذا بدوره يفتح فهمًا جديدًا للوحي الإلهي الذي قد يقدم إجابة للأسئلة التي يواجهها الجميع يوميًا في تجاربهم ومحنهم الشخصية.

Allah opens the path to knowledge when we start using reason when reading the Quran This is turn opens a new understanding on Allahs's divine revelation which may provide answer to the questions everyone is facing daily in their own personal trials and tribulations.

Hadith on Reciting the Quran in seven different ways

عن عمر بن الخطاب رضي الله عنه: سمعت هشام بن حكيم يقرأ سورة الفرقان في حياة رسول الله صلى الله عليه وسلم.

وسمعت قراءته فرأيت أنه قرأه على حروف كثيرة لم يعلمنيها رسول الله صلى الله عليه وسلم. فأردت أن أقفز عليه وهو يصلي، فانتظرت حتى قضى الصلاة، فأخذته بإزاره أو بإزاري، فقلت له: من علمك قراءة هذه السورة؟

قال: علمني رسول الله صلى الله عليه وسلم كيف أقرأها. فقلت له: كذبت، والله لقد علمني رسول الله صلى الله عليه وسلم هذه السورة التي سمعتك تقرأها.

فانطلقت أقوده إلى رسول الله صلى الله عليه وسلم. قلت: يا رسول الله، سمعت هذا الرجل يقرأ سورة الفرقان بما لم تعلمنيه، وعلمتني كيف أقرأها.

فقال رسول الله صلى الله عليه وسلم: «يا عمر دعه، اقرأ يا هشام». فقرأ هشام بين يديه كما سمعته يقرأ

فقال رسول الله صلى الله عليه وسلم: «هكذا نزلت». فقال رسول الله صلى الله عليه وسلم: «اقرأ يا عمر». لذلك قرأته

فقال النبي صلى الله عليه وسلم: «هكذا نزلت». ثم أضاف: «إن هذا القرآن نزل على سبعة أحرف، فاقرأوه على ما تيسر منه».

رواه البخاري ومسلم

Umar ibn al-Khattab (May Allah be pleased with him) reported: I heard Hisham ibn Hakim recite Surat al-Furqan during the lifetime of the Messenger of Allah (May Allah's peace and blessings be upon him).

I listened to his recitation and noticed that he recited it in many ways which the Messenger of Allah (May Allah's peace and blessings be upon him) had not taught me. So, I was about to jump upon him during the prayer, but I waited till he finished the prayer, whereupon I seized him by either his upper garment or mine and asked him: "Who taught you how to recite this Surah?"

He replied: "The Messenger of Allah (May Allah's peace and blessings be upon him) taught me how to recite it." So, I said to him: "You have told a lie! By Allah, the Messenger of Allah (May Allah's peace and blessings be upon him) taught me this Surah which I have heard you recite."

So, I set forth, leading him to the Messenger of Allah (May Allah's peace and blessings be upon him). I said: "O the Messenger of Allah, I heard this man recite Surat al-Furqan in ways which you have not taught me, and you taught me how to recite it."

On that, the Messenger of Allah (May Allah's peace and blessings be upon him) said: "O Umar, let go of him! Recite, O Hisham." So Hisham recited before him in the way I had heard him recite.

The Messenger of Allah (May Allah's peace and blessings be upon him) said: "It was revealed like this." Then the Messenger of Allah (May Allah's peace and blessings be upon him) said: "Recite, O Umar!" So, I recited it.

The Prophet (May Allah's peace and blessings be upon him) said: "It was revealed like this." And then he added: *"Indeed, this Qur'an has been revealed in seven different ways, so recite it in the way that is easy for you."*

Narrated by Al-Bukhari as well as Muslim

حديث عن ثواب قراءة القرآن

Hadith on Reward for reciting the Quran

قال (رضي الله عنه) Muhammad bin Ka'b Al-Qurazi :(

سمعت عبد الله بن مسعود رضي الله عنه يقول: قال رسول الله صلى الله عليه وسلم:

من قرأ حرفاً من كتاب الله فله حسنه وثواب عشرة أمثاله. ولا أقول ألف لام **ااا** حرف ولكن ألف حرف ولام حرف وميم حرف.

رواه الترمذي

Muhammad bin Ka'b Al-Qurazi (May Allah be pleased with him) said:

"I heard Abdullah bin Masud (May Allah be pleased with him) saying: The Messenger of Allah (May the peace and blessings of Allah be upon him) said:

"Whoever recites a letter from Allah's Book, then he receives the reward from it, and the reward of ten the like of it. I do not say that Alif Lam Mim is a letter, but Alif is a letter, Lam is a letter and Mim is a letter.

Narrated by At-Tirmidhi

قالت عائشة (رضي الله عنها):(

قال النبي صلى الله عليه وسلم: «من قرأ القرآن وهو في حفظه كان مع السفرة الكرام البررة في الجنة. ومن اجتهد في حفظ القرآن، وقرأه بجهد شديد، كان له أجران».

«رواه البخاري»

Aisha (May Allah be pleased with her) said:

The Prophet (ﷺ) said, "Such a person as recites the Quran and masters it by heart, will be with the noble righteous scribes in Heaven.

And such a person exerts himself to learn the Quran by heart, and recites it with great difficulty, will have a double reward."
      Narrated by Al-Bukhari

أحاديث تخالف القرآن

Hadiths that contradict the Quran

يقدس المسلمون القرآن باعتباره المصدر الأساسي والصافي للوحي الإلهي. ولكن هناك من يؤكد أن هناك بعض الأحاديث التي تتعارض مع القرآن.

الأحاديث عموما مليئة بالتناقضات. وأي حديث يتناقض مع آية في القرآن ينبغي أن يؤخذ على محمل الجد. الآية التالية تنص على أنه لا يوجد تناقض في القرآن. والعكس صحيح بالنسبة للحديث

Muslims revere the Quran as the primary and pure source of divine revelations. There are however some that contend there are certain Hadiths that contradict the Quran.

Hadiths are generally full of contradictions. Any Hadith that contradicts a verse in the Quran should be taken seriously. The following verse states that there are no contradictions in the Quran. The opposite is true for Hadith.

(سورة النساء 4: 82)

أفلا يتدبرون القرآن؟ ولو كان من عند غير الله لوجدوا فيه اختلافا كثيرا.

Do they not then reflect on the Quran? Had it been from anyone other than Allah, they would have certainly found in it many inconsistencies.

الأحاديث التالية هي في تناقض كامل وكلي للقرآن. أثارت هذه التناقضات تساؤلات في المجتمع الإسلامي حول غرض الحديث وصحته بالنسبة للقرآن.

The following Hadiths are in complete and total contradiction of the Quran. These contradictions raised questions in the Muslim community about the purpose and authenticity of Hadith in relation to the Quran.

Hadith on Stoning

(سورة النور 2:24)

ٱلزَّانِيَةُ وَٱلزَّانِى فَٱجْلِدُوا۟ كُلَّ وَٰحِدٍ مِّنْهُمَا مِا۟ئَةَ جَلْدَةٍ ۖ وَلَا تَأْخُذْكُم بِهِمَا رَأْفَةٌ فِى دِينِ ٱللَّهِ إِن كُنتُمْ تُؤْمِنُونَ بِٱللَّهِ وَٱلْيَوْمِ ٱلْءَاخِرِ ۖ وَلْيَشْهَدْ عَذَابَهُمَا طَآئِفَةٌ مِّنَ ٱلْمُؤْمِنِينَ

As for female and male fornicators, give each of them one hundred lashes, and do not let pity for them make you lenient in enforcing the law of Allah, if you truly believe in Allah and the Last Day. And let a number of believers witness their punishment.

بدالله ب. وذكر عباس أن عمر ب. فجلس الخطاب على منبر رسول الله صلى الله عليه وسلم (عليه الصلاة والسلام) و قال:

حقا أرسل الله محمدا (عليه الصلاة والسلام) بالحق و أنزل عليه الكتاب وكانت آية الرجم فيما أنزل عليه.

قرأناه وحفظناه في ذاكرتنا وفهمناه. وقد قضى رسول الله صلى الله عليه وسلم بحد الرجم حتى الموت إلى الزاني المتزوج والزانية ومن بعده فرضنا الرجم.

وأخشى أن ينسى الناس مع مرور الزمن، فيقولوا: لا نجد حد الرجم في كتاب الله، فيضلوا بترك هذا الفريضة التي فرضها الله.

الرجم فريضة في كتاب الله على الزاني والمحصن إذا قامت البينة، أو كان هناك حمل، أو اعتراف.

رواه مسلم

Abdullah b. Abbas reported that Umar b. Khattab sat on the pulpit of Allah's Messenger (May the peace and blessing of Allah be upon him) and said:

Verily Allah sent Muhammad (May the peace and blessing of Allah be upon him) with truth and He sent down the Book upon him, and the verse of stoning was included in what was sent down to him.

We recited it, retained it in our memory and understood it. *Allah's Messenger (May the peace and blessing of Allah be upon him) awarded the punishment of stoning to death to the married adulterer and adulteress* and, after him, we also awarded the punishment of stoning.

I am afraid that with the lapse of time, the people may forget it and may say: We do not find the punishment of stoning in the Book of Allah, and thus go astray by abandoning this duty prescribed by Allah.

Stoning is a duty laid down in Allah's Book for married men and women who commit adultery when proof is established, or if there is pregnancy, or a confession.

Narrated by Muslim

كما يوضح القرآن عقوبة الزنا للعبد المتزوج وهي نصف عقوبة الزنا الحر المتزوج.

The Quran also clarifies the punishment for adultery for a married slave which is half of that of a free married person.

(سورة النساء 4:25)

وَمَن لَّمْ يَسْتَطِعْ مِنكُمْ طَوْلًا أَن يَنكِحَ ٱلْمُحْصَنَـٰتِ ٱلْمُؤْمِنَـٰتِ فَمِن مَّا مَلَكَتْ أَيْمَـٰنُكُم مِّن فَتَيَـٰتِكُمُ ٱلْمُؤْمِنَـٰتِ ۚ وَٱللَّهُ أَعْلَمُ بِإِيمَـٰنِكُم ۚ بَعْضُكُم مِّن بَعْضٍ ۚ فَٱنكِحُوهُنَّ بِإِذْنِ أَهْلِهِنَّ وَءَاتُوهُنَّ أُجُورَهُنَّ بِٱلْمَعْرُوفِ مُحْصَنَـٰتٍ غَيْرَ مُسَـٰفِحَـٰتٍ وَلَا مُتَّخِذَٰتِ أَخْدَانٍ ۚ فَإِذَآ أُحْصِنَّ فَإِنْ أَتَيْنَ بِفَـٰحِشَةٍ فَعَلَيْهِنَّ نِصْفُ مَا عَلَى ٱلْمُحْصَنَـٰتِ مِنَ ٱلْعَذَابِ ۚ ذَٰلِكَ لِمَنْ خَشِىَ ٱلْعَنَتَ مِنكُمْ ۚ وَأَن تَصْبِرُوا۟ خَيْرٌ لَّكُمْ ۗ وَٱللَّهُ غَفُورٌ رَّحِيمٌ

But if any of you cannot afford to marry a free believing woman, then let him marry a believing bondwoman possessed by one of you. Allah knows best the state of your faith and theirs.

You are from one another. So, marry them with the permission of their owners, giving them their dowry in fairness, if they are chaste, neither promiscuous nor having secret affairs.

If they commit indecency after marriage, they receive half the punishment of free women. *This is for those of you who fear falling into sin. But if you are patient, it is better for you. And Allah is All-Forgiving, Most Merciful.*

حديث عن الشفاعة

Hadith on Intercession

(سورة الزمر 39:44)

قُل لِّلَّهِ ٱلشَّفَٰعَةُ جَمِيعًا ۖ لَّهُۥ مُلۡكُ ٱلسَّمَٰوَٰتِ وَٱلۡأَرۡضِ ۖ ثُمَّ إِلَيۡهِ تُرۡجَعُونَ

Say, "*All intercession belongs to Allah alone.* To Him belongs the kingdom of the heavens and the earth. Then to Him you will all be returned.".

عبدالله ب. عمرو ب. العاص رضي الله عنه أن رسول الله صلى الله عليه وسلم قال:

فإذا سمعتم المؤذن فقولوا مثل ما يقول، ثم صلوا علي، فإنه من صلى علي صلاة صلى الله عليه بها عشرا؛ فاسأل الله لي الوسيلة، فإنها درجة في الجنة لا ينبغي إلا لعبد من عباد الله، وأرجو أن أكون هو ذلك.

ومن سألني الوسيلة حققت له شفاعتي.

رواه مسلم

Abdullah b. Amr b. al-As (May Allah be pleased with him) reported Allah's Messenger (May the peace and blessings of Allah be upon him) saying:

When you hear the Mu'adhdhin, repeat what he says, then invoke a blessing on me, for everyone who invokes a blessing on me will receive ten blessings from Allah; then beg from Allah al-Wasila for me, which is a rank in Paradise fitting for only one of Allah's servants, and I hope that I may be that one.

If anyone asks that I be given the Wasila, he will be assured of my intercession.

Narrated by Muslim

حديث عن غزارة الماء

Hadith on Water Gushing

(سورة الإسراء 17: 90-93)

وَقَالُوا۟ لَن نُّؤْمِنَ لَكَ حَتَّىٰ تَفْجُرَ لَنَا مِنَ ٱلْأَرْضِ يَنۢبُوعًا أَوْ تَكُونَ لَكَ جَنَّةٌ مِّن نَّخِيلٍ وَعِنَبٍ فَتُفَجِّرَ ٱلْأَنْهَٰرَ خِلَٰلَهَا تَفْجِيرًا

أرض, أو أن تكون لك جنة من نخيل و كروم فتجري الأنهار فيها تفجير أَوْ تُسْقِطَ ٱلسَّمَآءَ كَمَا زَعَمْتَ عَلَيْنَا كِسَفًا أَوْ تَأْتِىَ بِٱللَّهِ وَٱلْمَلَٰٓئِكَةِ قَبِيلًا أَوْ يَكُونَ لَكَ بَيْتٌ مِّن زُخْرُفٍ أَوْ تَرْقَىٰ فِى ٱلسَّمَآءِ وَلَن نُّؤْمِنَ لِرُقِيِّكَ حَتَّىٰ تُنَزِّلَ عَلَيْنَا كِتَٰبًا نَّقْرَؤُهُۥ ۗ قُلْ سُبْحَانَ رَبِّى هَلْ كُنتُ إِلَّا بَشَرًا رَّسُولًا

*They challenge the Prophet, "**We will never believe in you until you cause a spring to gush forth from the earth for us**, or until you have a garden of palm trees and vineyards, and cause rivers to flow abundantly in it, or cause the sky to fall upon us in pieces, as you have claimed, or bring Allah and the angels before us, face to face or until you have a house of gold, or you ascend into heaven—and even then, we will not believe in your ascension until you bring down to us a book that we can read." Say, **"Glory be to my Lord! Am I not only a human messenger?***

(عن سالم بن أبي الجد (رضي الله عنه):

وعن جابر بن عبد الله قال: اشتد العطش يوم الحديبية، وكان بين يدي النبي صلى الله عليه وسلم قدر فيه ماء. (عليه الصلاة والسلام) فلما فرغ من الوضوء اندفع الناس إليه.

فقال: ما بك؟ فقالوا: ليس عندنا ماء للوضوء ولا للشرب إلا ما بين يديك. فوضع يده في ذلك القدر فجعل الماء يتدفق بين أصابعه كالينابيع.

فشربنا وتوضأنا منه، فقلت لجابر: كم كنتم؟ قال: لو كنا مائة ألف لكفانا، ولكن كنا 1500

رواه البخاري

Salim bin Abi Aj-Jad (May Allah be pleased with him) narrated: Jabir bin Abdullah said, "The people became very thirsty on the day of Al-Hudaibiya (Treaty). A small pot containing some water was in front of the Prophet (May the peace and blessing of Allah be upon him) and when he had finished the ablution, the people rushed towards him.

He asked, "What is wrong with you?" They replied, "We have no water either for performing ablution or for drinking except what is present in front of you." *So, he placed his hand in that pot and the water started flowing among his fingers like springs.*

We all drank and performed ablution from it." I asked Jabir, "How many were you?" he replied, "Even if we had been one hundred thousand, it would have been sufficient for us, but we were fifteen hundred."

Narrated by Al- Bukhari

Hadith on Reason

(سورة الأنفال 8:22)

إِنَّ شَرَّ ٱلدَّوَآبِّ عِندَ ٱللَّهِ ٱلصُّمُّ ٱلْبُكْمُ ٱلَّذِينَ لَا يَعْقِلُونَ

*Indeed, the worst of all beings in the sight of Allah are the **willfully deaf and dumb, who do not understand.***

عن جندب رضي الله عنه:

قال النبي (صلى الله عليه وسلم): ومن فسر كتاب الله برأيه ولو كان على حق فقد أخطأ.

رواه أبو داود

Jundub (May Allah be pleased with him) narrated:

The Prophet (May the peace and blessings of Allah be upon him) said: *If anyone interprets the Book of Allah in the light of his opinion even if he is right, he has erred.*

Narrated by Abu Dawud

الحديث على الردة

Hadith on Apostasy

ولم يذكر القرآن أي عقوبة في الأرض على من يرتد عن المعتقدات الدينية، بل يؤجلها إلى الحياة الآخرة.

The Quran does not mention any punishment on earth for the renouncing of religious beliefs but rather postpones it to the afterlife.

(سورة النساء 4: 136-137)

يَـٰٓأَيُّهَا ٱلَّذِينَ ءَامَنُوٓا۟ ءَامِنُوا۟ بِٱللَّهِ وَرَسُولِهِۦ وَٱلْكِتَـٰبِ ٱلَّذِى نَزَّلَ عَلَىٰ رَسُولِهِۦ وَٱلْكِتَـٰبِ ٱلَّذِىٓ أَنزَلَ مِن قَبْلُ وَمَن يَكْفُرْ بِٱللَّهِ وَمَلَـٰٓئِكَتِهِۦ وَكُتُبِهِۦ وَرُسُلِهِۦ وَٱلْيَوْمِ ٱلْـَٔاخِرِ فَقَدْ ضَلَّ ضَلَـٰلًۢا بَعِيدًا

إِنَّ ٱلَّذِينَ ءَامَنُوا۟ ثُمَّ كَفَرُوا۟ ثُمَّ ءَامَنُوا۟ ثُمَّ كَفَرُوا۟ ثُمَّ ٱزْدَادُوا۟ كُفْرًا لَّمْ يَكُنِ ٱللَّهُ لِيَغْفِرَ لَهُمْ وَلَا لِيَهْدِيَهُمْ سَبِيلًۢا

O believers! Have faith in Allah, His Messenger, the Book He has revealed to His Messenger, and the Scriptures He revealed before.

Indeed, whoever denies Allah, His angels, His Books, His messengers, and the Last Day has clearly gone far astray.

Indeed, those who believed then disbelieved, then believed and again disbelieved only increasing in disbelief. Allah will neither forgive them nor guide them to the Right Way.

:وعن عكرمة رضي الله عنه

لقد أحرق علي أناساً، فبلغ هذا الخبر ابن عباس، فقال: لو كنت مكانه ما أحرقتهم، كما قال النبي صلى الله عليه وسلم: (عليه الصلاة والسلام) قال لا تعذبوا أحداً بعذاب الله». لا شك أني قتلتهم من أجل النبي (عليه الصلاة والسلام) قال، «من يرتد عن دينه فاقتلوه».

رواه البخاري

Ikrima (May Allah be pleased with him) narrated:

Ali burnt some people and this news reached Ibn Abbas, who said, "Had I been in his place I would not have burnt them, as the Prophet (May the peace and blessing of Allah be upon him) said,

"Don't punish anybody with Allah's Punishment." No doubt, I would have killed them, for the Prophet (May the peace and blessing of Allah be upon him) said, *"If somebody (a Muslim) discards his religion, kill him."*

Narrated by Al- Bukhari

الفصل الرابع
الوحي غير القرآن

CHAPTER FOUR
Revelation other than the Quran

(سورة المائدة 5:92)

وَأَطِيعُوا۟ ٱللَّهَ وَأَطِيعُوا۟ ٱلرَّسُولَ وَٱحْذَرُوا۟ۚ فَإِن تَوَلَّيْتُمْ فَٱعْلَمُوٓا۟ أَنَّمَا عَلَىٰ رَسُولِنَا ٱلْبَلَٰغُ ٱلْمُبِينُ

Obey Allah and obey the Messenger and beware! *But if you turn away, then know that Our Messenger's duty is only to deliver the message clearly*

(سورة الحاقة 69: 44-47)

وَلَوْ تَقَوَّلَ عَلَيْنَا بَعْضَ ٱلْأَقَاوِيلِ لَأَخَذْنَا مِنْهُ بِٱلْيَمِينِ ثُمَّ لَقَطَعْنَا مِنْهُ ٱلْوَتِينَ فَمَا مِنكُم مِّنْ أَحَدٍ عَنْهُ حَٰجِزِينَ

Had the Messenger made up something in Our Name, ***We would have certainly seized him by his right hand, then severed his aorta,*** *and none of you could have shielded him from Us!*

.وقد أمرنا الله بطاعة الرسول، و أنذرنا أنه إذا اختلق شيئاً في سبيل الله سيموت

Allah commands us to obey the Messenger and warns that if he made up anything in Allah's name he would die.

(Surah Al-Jinn 72:26-28)

عَٰلِمُ ٱلْغَيْبِ فَلَا يُظْهِرُ عَلَىٰ غَيْبِهِۦٓ أَحَدًا إِلَّا مَنِ ٱرْتَضَىٰ مِن رَّسُولٍ فَإِنَّهُۥ يَسْلُكُ مِنۢ بَيْنِ يَدَيْهِ وَمِنْ خَلْفِهِۦ رَصَدًا لِّيَعْلَمَ أَن قَدْ أَبْلَغُوا۟ رِسَٰلَٰتِ رَبِّهِمْ وَأَحَاطَ بِمَا لَدَيْهِمْ وَأَحْصَىٰ كُلَّ شَىْءٍ عَدَدًۢا

He is the Knower of the unseen, disclosing none of it to anyone, except messengers of His choice. *Then He appoints angel-guards before*

and behind them to ensure that the messengers fully deliver the messages of their Lord—though He already knows all about them, and keeps account of everything."

تسلط الآية أعلاه الضوء على حقيقة أن الله، إلى جانب تنزيل الكتب المقدسة، أنزل أيضًا رسائل على الرسل.

آيات الله تعالى تتكلم عن سنة رسول الله صلى الله عليه وسلم

وقد نزل على رسول الله صلى الله عليه وسلم آيات أخرى لم يرد ذكرها في القرآن. الآيات التالية تثبت بوضوح الوحي غير القرآن وتقدم دليلا لمن يرفض الحديث.

The above verse highlights the fact that Allah besides revealing the Scriptures also revealed messages to the Messengers.

The divine revelations of Allah speak to the Sunnah of the Messenger of Allah (May the blessings and peace of Allah be upon him)

The Messenger of Allah (May the peace and blessings of Allah be upon him) received other Revelations that are not mentioned in the Quran. The following verses clearly proves Revelations other than the Quran and provides evidence to anyone who rejects Hadith.

زوجات النبي

The Prophet's Wives

(سورة التحريم 66: 3)

وَإِذْ أَسَرَّ ٱلنَّبِىُّ إِلَىٰ بَعْضِ أَزْوَٰجِهِ حَدِيثًا فَلَمَّا نَبَّأَتْ بِهِ وَأَظْهَرَهُ ٱللَّهُ عَلَيْهِ عَرَّفَ بَعْضَهُ وَأَعْرَضَ عَن بَعْضٍ فَلَمَّا نَبَّأَهَا بِهِ قَالَتْ مَنْ أَنۢبَأَكَ هَـٰذَا قَالَ نَبَّأَنِىَ ٱلْعَلِيمُ ٱلْخَبِيرُ

فلما أخبرها بذلك قالت: من أخبرك بهذا؟ رد، "بلغني العليم الخبير."

*Remember when the Prophet had once confided something to one of his wives, then when she disclosed it to another wife and **Allah made it known to him**, he presented to her part of what was disclosed and overlooked a part*

*So, when he informed her of it, she exclaimed, "Who told you this?" He replied, "**I was informed by the All-Knowing, All-Aware.**"*

والآية السابقة تدل على أن الله أعطى الوحي النبوي منفصل عن القرآن. وقد نزل هذا على النبي عندما كشفت إحدى زوجاته التي أسرها بالخبر لزوجة أخرى. ولا توجد آية أخرى في القرآن يخبر فيها الله النبي بكشف زوجته للآخر. وهذا يعني أن النبي تلقى الوحي من الله مستقلاً عن القرآن.

The above verse indicates that ***Allah gave the Prophet revelation separately from the Quran.*** This was revealed to the Prophet when one of his wives whom he confided in disclosed the information to another wife. ***There is no other verse in the Quran where Allah informs the Prophet about his wife's disclosure to the other.*** This means that the Prophet received revelation from Allah independent from the Quran.

ثلاثة آلاف ملائكة

Three Thousand Angels

(سورة علي عمران 124 : 3)

وتذكر أيها النبي إذ قلت للمؤمنين أو لا يكفي ذلك فينزل ربكم مدداً من ثلاثة آلاف من الملائكة ينصرونكم؟"

Remember, O Prophet, when you said to the believers, "Is it not enough that your Lord will send down a reinforcement of three thousand angels for your aid?"

والسؤال الذي يجب طرحه هو: أين قال الله في القرآن: سيؤيد المؤمنين بثلاثة آلاف من الملائكة؟ لا يوجد مثل هذه الآية في القرآن. والآية أعلاه تثبت أن النبي تلقى وحيا آخر من الله منفصلا عن القرآن.

The question that needs to be asked is *"Where did Allah say in the Quran He will reinforce the believers with three thousand angels?"* There is no such verse in the Quran. The above verse proves that the Prophet received another revelation from Allah separate from the Quran.

جواز الجماع في ليلة الصيام

Permissibilty of Intimacy on the night before the Fast

(سورة البقرة 2: 187)

أُحِلَّ لَكُمْ لَيْلَةَ ٱلصِّيَامِ ٱلرَّفَثُ إِلَىٰ نِسَآئِكُمْ هُنَّ لِبَاسٌ لَّكُمْ وَأَنتُمْ لِبَاسٌ لَّهُنَّ عَلِمَ ٱللَّهُ أَنَّكُمْ كُنتُمْ تَخْتَانُونَ أَنفُسَكُمْ فَتَابَ عَلَيْكُمْ وَعَفَا عَنكُمْ فَٱلْـَٰنَ بَـٰشِرُوهُنَّ وَٱبْتَغُوا مَا كَتَبَ ٱللَّهُ لَكُمْ وَكُلُوا وَٱشْرَبُوا حَتَّىٰ يَتَبَيَّنَ لَكُمُ ٱلْخَيْطُ ٱلْأَبْيَضُ مِنَ ٱلْخَيْطِ ٱلْأَسْوَدِ مِنَ ٱلْفَجْرِ ثُمَّ أَتِمُّوا ٱلصِّيَامَ إِلَى ٱلَّيْلِ وَلَا تُبَـٰشِرُوهُنَّ وَأَنتُمْ عَـٰكِفُونَ فِى ٱلْمَسَـٰجِدِ تِلْكَ حُدُودُ ٱللَّهِ فَلَا تَقْرَبُوهَا كَذَٰلِكَ يُبَيِّنُ ٱللَّهُ ءَايَـٰتِهِ لِلنَّاسِ لَعَلَّهُمْ يَتَّقُونَ

It has been made permissible for you to be intimate with your wives during the nights preceding the fast. Your spouses are a garment for you as you are for them.

Allah knows that you were deceiving yourselves. So, He has accepted your repentance and pardoned you. So now you may be intimate with them and seek what Allah has prescribed for you..

كشف الآية أعلاه أن الله يعلم أنكم تخادعون أنفسكم، وقد أجاز لكم ممارسة الجنس مع زوجاتكم في الليالي التي تسبق الصيام.

لا يوجد أمر أول في القرآن أن الله قال أنه لا يجوز لك ممارسة الجنس أثناء الليل قبل الصيام. والآية أعلاه تثبت أيضاً أن النبي تلقى من الله وحياً غير مذكور في القرآن.

The above verse reveals that Allah knows that you are deceiving yourselves and has now made it permissible for you to be intimate with your wives during the nights preceding the fast.

There is no first command in the Quran that Allah said that you are not allowed to be intimate during the night preceding the fast. The above verse also proves that the Prophet received revelation from Allah not mentioned in the Quran.

تغيير اتجاه القبلة

Change of direction of Qibla

(سورة البقرة 2: 143-144)

وكذلك جعلناكم المؤمنين أمة قائمة لتكونوا شهداء على الناس ويكون الرسول عليكم شهيدا.

لقد عينا اتجاهك السابق للصلاة فقط لتمييز أولئك الذين سيبقون مخلصين للرسول من أولئك الذين سيفقدون الإيمان.

إنا نراك أيها النبي تتجه بوجهك نحو السماء. والآن سوف نوجهك نحو اتجاه الصلاة الذي يرضيك.

فول وجهك شطر المسجد الحرام بمكة وحيثما كنتم فولوا وجوهكم شطره. إن الذين أوتوا الكتاب ليعلمون أنه الحق من ربهم. وما الله بغافل عما يفعلون.

And so, We have made you believers an upright community so that you may be witnesses over humanity and that the Messenger may be a witness over you.

We assigned your former direction of prayer *only to distinguish those who would remain faithful to the Messenger from those who would lose faith.*

Indeed, We see you O Prophet turning your face towards heaven. ***Now We will make you turn towards a direction of prayer that will please you. So, turn your face towards the Sacred Mosque in Mecca—wherever you are, turn your faces towards it.*** *Those who were given the Scripture certainly know this to be the truth from their Lord. And Allah is never unaware of what they do.*

وتدل الآية على حدوث تحول في القبلة. وانتقلت القبلة الجديدة من القدس إلى المسجد الحرام. الأمر الأصلي لمواجهة القدس غير موجود في القرآن.

والسؤال الذي يجب أن يطرح هو: كيف عرف رسول الله صلى الله عليه وسلم مكان القبلة الأولى ولم يوجد أمر في القرآن؟ كما أنه لا يوجد وصف للقبلة الأولى أو أمر باتباع قبلة مختلفة قبل مكة في القرآن.

The verse reflects there was a shift in Qibla. The new Qibla moved from Jerusalem to Masjid al-Haram. ***The original command to face Jerusalem is not found in the Quran.***

The question that needs to be asked is "How did the Messenger of Allah (May the peace and blessings of Allah be upon him) know where the first Qibla was as there is no command in the Quran?" There is also ***no description of the first Qibla or a command to follow a different Qibla before Mecca in the Quran.***

حكمة

The Hikmah (Wisdom)

(سورة البقرة 2: 129)

*Our Lord! Raise from among them a messenger who will recite to them Your revelations, **teach them the Book and wisdom**, and purify them. Indeed, You alone are the Almighty, All-Wise.*

(Surah An-Nahl 16:44)

أرسلناهم بالبينات والكتب الإلهية .وأنزلنا إليك أيها النبي الذكر لتبين للناس ما نزل لهم ولعلهم يتفكرون.

*We sent them with clear proofs and divine Books. **And We have sent down to you O Prophet the Reminder, so that you may explain to people what has been revealed for them, and perhaps they will reflect.***

الحكمة ليست القرآن لأن النبي يحتاج إلى أن يعلم المؤمنين شيئا آخر غير القرآن. وقد أخبر النبي أن يبين للناس السنة حتى يتفكروا. وبالتالي فإن الحكمة هي سنة النبي.

The Hikmah is not the Quran as the Prophet needs to teach the believers something other than the Quran. *The Prophet was informed to explain to people the Sunnah so that they can reflect. The Hikmah is therefore the Sunnah of the Prophet.*

الفصل الخامس
الأنبياء والرسل

CHAPTER FIVE
Prophets and Messengers

(سورة آل عمران 3: 81)

تذكر عندما وأخذ الله ميثاق الأنبياء فقال: "والآن بعد أن آتيتكم الكتاب والحكمة"،
"فإذا جاءكم رسول مصدق لما معكم لتؤمنوا به وتنصروه".
وأضاف: هل تؤكدون هذا العهد وتقبلون هذا الالتزام؟ قالوا: نعم. قال الله: فاشهدوا
وأنا شهيد

Remember when Allah made a covenant with the Prophets saying
"Now that I have given you the Book and wisdom, if there comes to
you a Messenger confirming what you have, you must believe in him
and support him."

He added, "Do you affirm this covenant and accept this commitment?"
They said, ***"Yes, we do."*** Allah said, "Then bear witness, and I too am a
Witness.".

تخبرنا الآية أن الأنبياء (النبي) هم رسل (رسول) الله الذين تم تكليفهم بكتب مقدسة
جديدة. ومن ناحية أخرى، فإن الرسل ليسوا أنبياء، بل يؤكدون الكتب المقدسة
الموجودة ويوصلون الرسالة الإلهية إلى الناس.

ذكر الله خمسة وعشرين نبياً في القرآن، لكن الإجماع بين كثير من المسلمين على
أن هناك أنبياء آخرين لم يذكرهم الله. يعترف الإسلام بآدم وإبراهيم (إبراهيم)
وإسماعيل (إسماعيل) وموسى (موسى) وداود (داوود) وعيسى (يسوع) ومحمد
كأنبياء خمسة عظماء

كان لأنبياء الله ورسله وظائف مختلفة حيث ذكر الله الأنبياء والرسل في آيتين مختلفتين في القرآن. أمرنا الله أن لا نفرق بين الأنبياء.

The verse informs us that Prophets (Nabi) are Messengers (Rasul) of Allah who are entrusted with new scriptures. Messengers on the other hand are not Prophets but confirm the existing scriptures and deliver the divine message to the people.

Allah mentions twenty-five Prophets in the Quran but the consensus amongst many Muslims is that there were also other Prophets Allah did not mention. Islam recognises Adam, Ebrahim (Abraham), Isma'il (Ishmael), Musa (Moses), Dawud (David), Isa (Jesus) and Muhammad as the five great Prophets.

The Prophets and Messengers of Allah had different functions as Allah mentions the Prophets and Messenger in two distinct different verses in the Quran. Allah commands us not to make a distinction between the Prophets.

(سورة البقرة 2:136)

قُولُوٓاْ ءَامَنَّا بِٱللَّهِ وَمَآ أُنزِلَ إِلَيْنَا وَمَآ أُنزِلَ إِلَىٰٓ إِبْرَٰهِۦمَ وَإِسْمَٰعِيلَ وَإِسْحَٰقَ وَيَعْقُوبَ وَٱلْأَسْبَاطِ وَمَآ أُوتِىَ مُوسَىٰ وَعِيسَىٰ وَمَآ أُوتِىَ ٱلنَّبِيُّونَ مِن رَّبِّهِمْ لَا نُفَرِّقُ بَيْنَ أَحَدٍ مِّنْهُمْ وَنَحْنُ لَهُۥ مُسْلِمُونَ

*Say, O believers, "We believe in Allah and what has been revealed to us; and what was revealed to Abraham, Ishmael, Isaac, Jacob, and his descendants; and what was given to Moses, Jesus, and other prophets from their Lord. **We make no distinction between any of them**. And to Allah we all submit."*

(سورة علي عمران 3:84)

قُلْ ءَامَنَّا بِٱللَّهِ وَمَآ أُنزِلَ عَلَيْنَا وَمَآ أُنزِلَ عَلَىٰٓ إِبْرَٰهِيمَ وَإِسْمَٰعِيلَ وَإِسْحَٰقَ وَيَعْقُوبَ وَٱلْأَسْبَاطِ وَمَآ أُوتِىَ مُوسَىٰ وَعِيسَىٰ وَٱلنَّبِيُّونَ مِن رَّبِّهِمْ لَا نُفَرِّقُ بَيْنَ أَحَدٍ مِّنْهُمْ وَنَحْنُ لَهُۥ مُسْلِمُونَ

Say, O Prophet, "We believe in Allah and what has been revealed to us and what was revealed to Abraham, Ishmael, Isaac, Jacob, and his descendants; and what was given to Moses, Jesus, and other prophets from their

*Lord—**we make no distinction between any of them,** and to Him we fully submit."*

.ويأمرنا الله في آية أخرى ألا نفرق بين الرسل

Allah in another verse also commands us not to make a distinction between the Messengers.

(سورة البقرة 2:285)

ءَامَنَ ٱلرَّسُولُ بِمَآ أُنزِلَ إِلَيْهِ مِن رَّبِّهِ وَٱلْمُؤْمِنُونَ كُلٌّ ءَامَنَ بِٱللَّهِ وَمَلَٰئِكَتِهِ وَكُتُبِهِ وَرُسُلِهِ لَا نُفَرِّقُ بَيْنَ أَحَدٍ مِّن رُّسُلِهِ وَقَالُوا سَمِعْنَا وَأَطَعْنَا غُفْرَانَكَ رَبَّنَا وَإِلَيْكَ ٱلْمَصِيرُ

*The Messenger firmly believes in what has been revealed to him from his Lord, and so do the believers. They all believe in Allah, His angels, His Books, and His messengers. They proclaim, **"We make no distinction between any of His messengers."***

*And they say, "We hear and obey. We seek Your forgiveness, our Lord! And to You alone is the final return. **As for those who believe in Allah and His messengers—accepting all; rejecting none—He will surely give them their rewards.** And Allah is All-Forgiving, Most Merciful.*

يوضح الله مسؤولية الأنبياء والمرسلين ويريد من البشرية أن تفهم سياق الآيات القرآنية عندما يتعلق الأمر بالأنبياء والمرسلين. ويؤكد الله هذه النقطة بذكر الرسول والنبي منفصلين في الآية التالية.

Allah clarifies the responsibility of the Prophets and Messengers and wants mankind to understand the context of the Quranic verses when it comes to the Prophets and the Messengers. *Allah reinforces this point by mentioning the Messenger and Prophet separately in the following verse.*

(Surah Al-Hajj 22:52)

وَمَآ أَرْسَلْنَا مِن قَبْلِكَ مِن رَّسُولٍ وَلَا نَبِيٍّ إِلَّا إِذَا تَمَنَّىٰ أَلْقَى ٱلشَّيْطَٰنُ فِى أُمْنِيَّتِهِ فَيَنسَخُ ٱللَّهُ مَا يُلْقِى ٱلشَّيْطَٰنُ ثُمَّ يُحْكِمُ ٱللَّهُ ءَايَٰتِهِ وَٱللَّهُ عَلِيمٌ حَكِيمٌ

***Whenever We sent a Messenger or a Prophet** before you O Prophet and he recited Our revelations, Satan would influence people's understanding of his recitation.*

But eventually Allah would eliminate Satan's influence. Then Allah would firmly establish His revelations. And Allah is All-Knowing, All-Wise.

كل نبي رسول (رسول) وليس كل رسول نبي. ولم يقل الله أن محمداً خاتم الرسل بل خاتم الأنبياء.

Every Prophet (Nabi) is a Messenger (Rasul) but not every Messenger is a Prophet. *Allah did not say Muhammad is the seal of the Messengers but rather the seal of the Prophets.*

(سورة الأحزاب 33:40)

مَّا كَانَ مُحَمَّدٌ أَبَآ أَحَدٍ مِّن رِّجَالِكُمْ وَلَٰكِن رَّسُولَ ٱللَّهِ وَخَاتَمَ ٱلنَّبِيِّـۧنَ ۗ وَكَانَ ٱللَّهُ بِكُلِّ شَىْءٍ عَلِيمًا

Muhammad is not the father of any of your men, *but is the Messenger of Allah and the seal of the Prophets.* And Allah has perfect knowledge of all things.

ونتعلم من القرآن أن كل نبي رسول وليس كل رسول نبي. أرسل الله الأنبياء مثل موسى (التوراة)، وداود (المزامير)، وعيسى (الإنجيل)، ومحمد (القرآن) لتأكيد وإيصال الوحي الإلهي.

القرآن هو آخر كتاب أنزله الله على الناس، ومحمد هو خاتم الأنبياء.

We learn from the Quran that every Prophet is a Messenger but not every Messenger is a Prophet. Allah sent Prophets like Moses (Torah), David (Psalms), Jesus (Injeel) and Muhammad (Quran) to affirm and deliver divine revelations.

The Quran is the final scripture Allah sent down to mankind as Muhammad is the seal of the Prophets.

(سورة آل عمران 3:3)

نَزَّلَ عَلَيْكَ ٱلْكِتَٰبَ بِٱلْحَقِّ مُصَدِّقًا لِّمَا بَيْنَ يَدَيْهِ وَأَنزَلَ ٱلتَّوْرَٮٰةَ وَٱلْإِنجِيلَ

He has revealed to you O Prophet the Book in truth, confirming what came before it, as *He revealed the Torah and the Gospel.*

تم منح الرسل وظائف محددة لإكمالها دون تسليم كتاب مقدس جديد. ولذلك فإن الرسل يفوقون عدد الأنبياء. ولم يكن الله بحاجة إلى تسمية جميع الرسل في القرآن.

The Messengers were given specific functions to complete without delivering a new scripture. The Messengers therefore exceed the number of Prophets. Allah did not need to name all the Messengers in the Quran.

(سورة غافر 40:34)

لقد جاءكم يوسف من قبل بالبينات، وما زلتم في شك مما جاءكم به. فلما مات قلتم لن يبعث الله من بعده رسولا أبدا." وهكذا يترك الله كل معتدٍ ومريبٍ في ضلال.

*Joseph already came to you earlier with clear proofs, yet you never ceased to doubt what he came to you with. **When he died you said, "Allah will never send a messenger after him."** This is how Allah leaves every transgressor and doubter to stray.*

ويذكر القرآن كفر وشك الأمم والقبائل الذين يقولون إن الله لن يرسل رسولا بعد يوسف. وكانوا يظنون أن يوسف هو آخر المرسلين

ولم تكن أمة رسول الله آخر أمة بعث الله رسولا منها. والآيات التالية ضمنية فيما يتعلق بهذه الحقيقة

The Quran mentions the disbelief and doubt of nations and tribes who say Allah will never send another Messenger after Joseph died. They thought that Joseph was the last Messenger.

The Ummah of the Messenger of Allah was not the last nation that Allah sent a Messenger. The following verses is implicit regarding this fact.

(سورة النساء 164: 4)

هناك رسل قد قصصنا عليك قصصهم وآخرون لم نقصصهم. وتكلم الله مع موسى مباشرة.

There are messengers whose stories We have told you already and others We have not. *And to Moses Allah spoke directly*

(سورة يونس 10:47)

وَلِكُلِّ أُمَّةٍ رَّسُولٌ ۖ فَإِذَا جَاءَ رَسُولُهُمْ قُضِيَ بَيْنَهُم بِالْقِسْطِ وَهُمْ لَا يُظْلَمُونَ

And for every nation there is a messenger. *After their messenger has come, judgment is passed on them in all fairness, and they are not wronged.*

الله يخاطب جميع الأمم إلى الأبد حيث سيتم إرسال الرسل إلى كل أمة على وجه الأرض لتلقي الهداية الإلهية.

كما تنص هذه الآية على أن الرسل أحياء عند تبليغ رسالة الله. وهذا يناقض القول بأن محمداً كان آخر رسول الله.

Allah addresses all nations until eternity *where Messengers will be sent to every nation on Earth to receive His divine guidance.*

This verse also states that the Messengers are alive when delivering Allah's message. This contradicts the contention that Muhammad was the last Messenger of Allah.

(سورة الأحقاف 46:9)

يقول، "لست أول رسول مرسل، ولا أعلم ماذا سيحدث لي أو لك. إن أتبع إلا ما يوحى إلي. وما بعثت إلا بنذير مبين».

Say, "*I am not the first messenger ever sent, nor do I know what will happen to me or you*. I only follow what is revealed to me. And I am only sent with a clear warning."

الفصل السادس
كتاب الله الواحد

CHAPTER SIX
Allahs One Book

عتبر القرآن والإنجيل والتوراة وحيًا إلهيًا، ويحتوي كل منها على روايات وتعاليم فريدة ويشترك في الإيمان المشترك بالتوحيد.

القرآن الذي يعتقد أنه الكتاب النهائي من عند الله يؤكد الوحي الإلهي للإنجيل والتوراة. كما يأمر القرآن المؤمنين باحترام هذه الكتب المقدسة على الرغم من ارتباطها بأنبياء مختلفين ونزلها بلغات مختلفة.

تم فهم وتفسير الروايات والتعاليم التي كانت عربية للقرآن، واليونانية للأناجيل، والعبرية للتوراة، وتفسيرها في سياق التقاليد الدينية الخاصة بكل منهم.

ويحكم الله على الذين لم يحكموا بما أنزل الله ثلاثة. الأول: أنهم كفار، والثاني ظالمون، والثالث فاسقون.

The Quran, Gospel and Torah are all considered divine revelations, each containing unique narratives, teachings and sharing a common belief in monotheism.

The Quran which is believed to be the final scripture from Allah affirms the divine revelations of the Gospel and Torah. The Quran also instructs the believers to respect these scriptures even though they were associated with different Prophets and revealed in different languages.

The narratives and teachings which were Arabic for the Quran, Greek for the Gospels and Hebrew for the Torah were understood and interpreted within the context of their respective religious traditions.

Allah issues three judgments against those who do not judge in accordance by what Allah has revealed. The first is that they are unbelievers, the second are wrong-doers and the third are transgressors.

(سورة المائدة 5: 44-47)

إِنَّآ أَنزَلْنَا ٱلتَّوْرَىٰةَ فِيهَا هُدًى وَنُورٌ ۚ يَحْكُمُ بِهَا ٱلنَّبِيُّونَ ٱلَّذِينَ أَسْلَمُوا۟ لِلَّذِينَ هَادُوا۟ وَٱلرَّبَّٰنِيُّونَ وَٱلْأَحْبَارُ بِمَا ٱسْتُحْفِظُوا۟ مِن كِتَٰبِ ٱللَّهِ وَكَانُوا۟ عَلَيْهِ شُهَدَآءَ ۚ فَلَا تَخْشَوُا۟ ٱلنَّاسَ وَٱخْشَوْنِ وَلَا تَشْتَرُوا۟ بِـَٔايَٰتِى ثَمَنًا قَلِيلًا ۚ وَمَن لَّمْ يَحْكُم بِمَآ أَنزَلَ ٱللَّهُ فَأُو۟لَٰٓئِكَ هُمُ ٱلْكَٰفِرُونَ

Indeed, We revealed the Torah, containing guidance and light, *by which the prophets, who submitted themselves to Allah, made judgments for Jews.*

So too did the rabbis and scholars judge according to Allah's Book, with which they were entrusted and of which they were made keepers. So, do not fear the people; fear Me! Nor trade my revelations for a fleeting gain. ***And those who do not judge by what Allah has revealed are truly the disbelievers.***

.وتشير الآية إلى أنه يجب على اليهود أن يتبعوا التوراة التي فيها الهدى والنور

The verse highlights that the Jews must follow the Torah which contains guidance and light.

وَكَتَبْنَا عَلَيْهِمْ فِيهَآ أَنَّ ٱلنَّفْسَ بِٱلنَّفْسِ وَٱلْعَيْنَ بِٱلْعَيْنِ وَٱلْأَنفَ بِٱلْأَنفِ وَٱلْأُذُنَ بِٱلْأُذُنِ وَٱلسِّنَّ بِٱلسِّنِّ وَٱلْجُرُوحَ قِصَاصٌ ۚ فَمَن تَصَدَّقَ بِهِ فَهُوَ كَفَّارَةٌ لَّهُ ۚ وَمَن لَّمْ يَحْكُم بِمَآ أَنزَلَ ٱللَّهُ فَأُو۟لَٰٓئِكَ هُمُ ٱلظَّٰلِمُونَ

وَقَفَّيْنَا عَلَىٰٓ ءَاثَٰرِهِم بِعِيسَى ٱبْنِ مَرْيَمَ مُصَدِّقًا لِّمَا بَيْنَ يَدَيْهِ مِنَ ٱلتَّوْرَىٰةِ ۖ وَءَاتَيْنَٰهُ ٱلْإِنجِيلَ فِيهِ هُدًى وَنُورٌ وَمُصَدِّقًا لِّمَا بَيْنَ يَدَيْهِ مِنَ ٱلتَّوْرَىٰةِ وَهُدًى وَمَوْعِظَةً لِّلْمُتَّقِينَ

We ordained for them in the Torah*, "A life for a life, an eye for an eye, a nose for a nose, an ear for an ear, a tooth for a tooth—and for wounds equal retaliation." But whoever waives it charitably, it will be atonement for them.* ***And those who do not judge by what Allah has revealed are truly the wrongdoers.***

Then in the footsteps of the prophets, We sent Jesus, son of Mary, confirming the Torah revealed before him. ***And We gave him the Gospel containing***

guidance and light and confirming what was revealed in the Torah—a guide and a lesson to the God-fearing.

يأمر الله المسيحيين باتباع الإنجيل ويؤكد أيضًا ما جاء في التوراة. ولم يذكر الله أن المسيحيين يجب أن يتبعوا القرآن.

Allah is telling the Christians to follow the Gospel and also confirms the revelations in the Torah. Allah does not mention that the Christians must follow the Quran.

وَلْيَحْكُمْ أَهْلُ ٱلْإِنجِيلِ بِمَآ أَنزَلَ ٱللَّهُ فِيهِ وَمَن لَّمْ يَحْكُم بِمَآ أَنزَلَ ٱللَّهُ فَأُوْلَٰئِكَ هُمُ ٱلْفَٰسِقُونَ

So, let the people of the Gospel judge by what Allah has revealed in it. **And those who do not judge by what Allah has revealed are truly the rebellious.**

الأنبياء لم ينكروا أي نبي قبلهم. وقد أكد كل نبي رسائل أسلافه. والله يؤيد ويصدق جميع الكتب السابقة التي أرسلها إلى الأنبياء.

The Prophets never denied any other Prophet that came before them. ***Each Prophet confirmed the messages of their predecessors.*** Allah supports and validates all the preceding Scriptures He sent to the Prophets.

(سورة النساء 4: 136)

يَٰٓأَيُّهَا ٱلَّذِينَ ءَامَنُوٓاْ ءَامِنُواْ بِٱللَّهِ وَرَسُولِهِ وَٱلْكِتَٰبِ ٱلَّذِى نَزَّلَ عَلَىٰ رَسُولِهِ وَٱلْكِتَٰبِ ٱلَّذِىٓ أَنزَلَ مِن قَبْلُ وَمَن يَكْفُرْ بِٱللَّهِ وَمَلَٰٓئِكَتِهِ وَكُتُبِهِ وَرُسُلِهِ وَٱلْيَوْمِ ٱلْءَاخِرِ فَقَدْ ضَلَّ ضَلَٰلًا بَعِيدًا

O believers! Have faith in Allah, His Messenger, the Book He has revealed to His Messenger, **and the Scriptures He revealed before.** *Indeed, whoever denies Allah, His angels, His Books, His messengers, and the Last Day has clearly gone far astray.*

النبي (عليه الصلاة والسلام) وجاء لبيان آيات التوراة والإنجيل. أمر الله المؤمنين أن يؤمنوا بما أنزل من قبل. ولكن هناك مسلمين لا يتبعون أمر الله لأنهم لا يؤمنون بالتوراة والإنجيل.

The Prophet (May the peace and blessings of Allah be upon him) came to clarify the verses of the Torah and the Gospel. ***Allah commands the believers to believe in the Scriptures He sent before.*** There are however Muslims that do not follow Allah's command as they don't believe in the Torah and Gospel.

(سورة العنكبوت 29:46)

وَلَا تُجَٰدِلُوٓا۟ أَهْلَ ٱلْكِتَٰبِ إِلَّا بِٱلَّتِى هِىَ أَحْسَنُ إِلَّا ٱلَّذِينَ ظَلَمُوا۟ مِنْهُمْ وَقُولُوٓا۟ ءَامَنَّا بِٱلَّذِىٓ أُنزِلَ إِلَيْنَا وَأُنزِلَ إِلَيْكُمْ وَإِلَٰهُنَا وَإِلَٰهُكُمْ وَٰحِدٌ وَنَحْنُ لَهُۥ مُسْلِمُونَ

Do not argue with the People of the Book unless gracefully, except with those of them who act wrongfully. And say, *"We believe in what has been revealed to us and what was revealed to you. Our God and your God is only One. And to Him we fully submit."*

يأمر الله المؤمنين أن لا يجادلوا أهل الكتاب وأن يحترمون كتبهم إلههم وإلهنا واحد

Allah is telling the believers not to argue with the people of the Book and to respect their scriptures as **their God and our God is One.**

(سورة المائدة 5:68)

قُلْ يَٰٓأَهْلَ ٱلْكِتَٰبِ لَسْتُمْ عَلَىٰ شَىْءٍ حَتَّىٰ تُقِيمُوا۟ ٱلتَّوْرَىٰةَ وَٱلْإِنجِيلَ وَمَآ أُنزِلَ إِلَيْكُم مِّن رَّبِّكُمْ وَلَيَزِيدَنَّ كَثِيرًا مِّنْهُم مَّآ أُنزِلَ إِلَيْكَ مِن رَّبِّكَ طُغْيَٰنًا وَكُفْرًا فَلَا تَأْسَ عَلَى ٱلْقَوْمِ ٱلْكَٰفِرِينَ

Say, O Prophet, "O People of the Book! **You have nothing to stand on unless you observe the Torah, the Gospel, and what has been revealed to you from your Lord."** *And your Lord's revelation to you O Prophet will only cause many of them to increase in wickedness and disbelief. So, do not grieve for the people who disbelieve.*

التوراة والإنجيل لا يمكن اعتبار هما منسوخين كما الله واضح جدا في ذلك ال ويجب مراعاة التوراة والإنجيل. وهذا لا يعني أن على المسلمين أن يتبعوا أحكام التوراة والإنجيل، بل أن يعترفوا بها ويعترفوا بها نعتقد أن الكتب المقدسة السابقة هي مصدر للوحي الإلهي.

The Torah and Gospel cannot be considered abrogated as Allah is very clear that **the Torah and Gospel must be observed.** This does not mean that Muslims must follow the laws of the Torah and Gospel but rather acknowledge and *believe that the previous scriptures are a source of divine revelations.*

(Surah Az-Zukhruf 43:3-4)

إِنَّا جَعَلْنَٰهُ قُرْءَٰنًا عَرَبِيًّا لَّعَلَّكُمْ تَعْقِلُونَ وَإِنَّهُۥ فِىٓ أُمِّ ٱلْكِتَٰبِ لَدَيْنَا لَعَلِىٌّ حَكِيمٌ

Certainly, We have made it a Quran in Arabic so perhaps you will understand. **And indeed, it is in the Master Record with Us** *highly esteemed, rich in wisdom.*

التوراة والأناجيل والقرآن كلها نسخ مختلفة لكتاب الله الواحد. قد لا يشارك جميع المؤمنين المسيحيين واليهود هذا الرأي لأن التفسيرات والمعتقدات يمكن أن تختلف داخل الدين.

ال السجل الرئيسي المذكورة في القرآن هي عند الله حيث أصل جميع الكتب المقدسة محفوظ.

The Torah, Gospels, and Quran are all different editions of Allah's One Book. This view might not be shared by all Christian and Jewish believers as interpretations and beliefs can vary within religion.

The *Master Record* mentioned in the Quran is *with Allah where the origin of all scriptures is preserved.*

www.ingramcontent.com/pod-product-compliance
Lightning Source LLC
Chambersburg PA
CBHW020625160726

47991CB00002BA/938